EMBRACING
the
COLD

A Guide to Solo Winter Travel
and Backcountry Expedition

THOM BARRETT

Copyright © 2024 by Thom Barrett

All rights reserved. No part of this book may be reproduced or used in any manner without written permission of the copyright owner except for the use of quotations in a book review. For more information, contact: Info@ livinglifewhiledying.com.

ISBN Paperback: 979-8-9909823-3-8
ISBN Electronic: 979-8-9909823-4-5
Library of Congress Control Number: 2024926377

Publishing Consultant: PRESStinely, PRESStinely.com

Portions of this book are works of nonfiction. Certain names and identifying characteristics have been changed.

Printed in the United States of America.

Thom Barrett
Living Life Press
www.livinglifewhiledying.com

Dedication

To those who hear the call of winter,
who see beauty where others see hardship,
and who find their truest selves in solitude.

To the trailblazers, the wanderers, and the dreamers—
may your journeys through the cold wilderness teach you strength,
patience, and reverence for the quiet magic of the natural world.

And to my family and friends, whose warmth
has been my constant shelter,
and to the wilderness itself, whose silence
has been my greatest teacher.

This book is for you.

—Thom Barrett

*"Winter doesn't reward those who merely endure it—
it favors those who respect its power, prepare for
its challenges, and embrace its beauty."*
—Thom Barrett

Preface

Embracing the Cold: A Guide to Solo Winter Travel and Backcountry Expedition is more than a checklist for winter camping—it's a comprehensive guide to thriving in the wilderness when the temperatures drop, the trails disappear, and the stakes are higher. Drawing from years of experience, this book dives deep into the physical preparation, mental resilience, and meticulous planning required to explore the backcountry solo in winter. Whether you are off for some peak-bagging or on an overlanding and off-roading adventure in winter, this book will help you prepare for your journey.

Winter demands respect, and this guide understands that challenge, offering practical advice on everything from securing your home before you leave to outfitting your vehicle for icy roads to choosing the right gear for camping and survival. You'll learn how to build physical strength and stamina to handle the relentless demands of trail-breaking in dense snow and how to manage the weight of a heavy pack over long distances. More importantly, you'll learn why physical endurance and mental resilience go hand in hand and how the proper training can keep you calm and focused when fatigue sets in.

The book also covers essential backcountry safety practices—crafting communication plans, preparing "exit strategies," and navigating with redundancy in case technology fails. There's a strong emphasis on wilderness first aid and emergency skills, with guidance on handling hypothermia, frostbite, and injuries in extreme conditions, as well as recommendations for training programs like wilderness first aid and avalanche safety courses offered by experts like NOLS, WMI, and SOLO.

Whether you're blazing a trail through untouched snow or simply looking to experience the solitude and beauty of winter in the backcountry, *Into the Winter Wild* offers the insights, tools, and mindset you'll need to approach the season's challenges with confidence. With thoughtful preparation, a respect for nature's power, and a commitment to safety at every step, winter can be more than an obstacle—it can be a place of quiet magic, profound discovery, and unmatched adventure.

Access Your Digital Resources

To help you prepare for your winter adventures, we've created comprehensive travel checklists that you can download to your phone or tablet. Simply scan the QR code below with your device's camera to access these essential planning tools. The checklists cover everything from gear inventory to vehicle preparation, helping you ensure nothing is overlooked as you prepare for your journey into the winter wilderness.

Can't scan the code? Visit www.livinglifewhiledying.com *to download the checklists directly.*

Contents

Dedication iii

Preface vii

Contents ix

Introduction: The Beauty of Winter xiii
    Adventure Trips xiv
    Sacred Journeys xiv
    Expeditions xv
    The Call of Winter xvi

Chapter 1: The Last Look Back – Preparing the Home 1
    Securing the Home 1
    Managing Utilities 3
    Preparing for Weather 3

Chapter 2: Machines and Ice – Equipping the Vehicle 5
    Bumper-to-Bumper Review of Both the Truck and the Jeep I Tow 5
    Cold Weather Tire Pressure Management 9
    Routine Checks and Maintenance Schedule 9
    Water Management in Freezing Conditions 10
    Ventilation, Safety, and CO/Propane Detection ... 10
    Portable Propane Heater for Backup Heat 11
    Fire Safety Precautions 12
    Managing Propane in Cold and High-Altitude Conditions 12
    Learning to Manage Power in Extreme Cold 13
    Navigation, Recovery, and Spare Gear 14
    Spare Tires and Repair Kit 15
    Solar Power for Off-Grid Living 15

Chapter 3: Off-Grid Essentials – Preparing for Boondocking 17
    Shelter and Insulation 17
    Food and Water Supplies 18
    Emergency and Safety Gear 19

Chapter 4: Layered for Survival – Dressing for Winter's Wrath 23
    The Layering System 24
    Important Considerations for Winter Clothing 26
    Staying Warm Around Camp 26

Chapter 5: The Real Fun – Gearing Up for Winter Adventures 29
    Snowshoes and Crampons 29
    Skis and Snowboarding Gear 30
    Backcountry Ski Essentials 30
        Additional Gear to Consider for Backcountry Skiing 31
    Snowmobile and Outer Gear 32
    Summary of Key Gear for Winter Adventures 32

Chapter 6: The Mental Game – Preparing for the Journey Ahead 35
    Do Your Homework: Research and Local Insight 35
    The Extra Caution of Solo Travel 36
    Balancing Safety and Solitude 37
    Building Mental Resilience 38
    Mental Health and Mindset Tips for Long Stretches of Solitude 38
    Final Thoughts on Winter Solitude 44

Chapter 7: Physical Conditioning and Health Preparation 47
    The Realities of Winter Terrain: Blazing New Trails 48
    The Weight of a Pack Over Time 49
    Building Mental Resilience Through Physical Training 50
    Pre-Trip Conditioning for Winter Backcountry Travel 50
    Preparing for Trail-Breaking and Adapting to Heavy Snow 52

Building Mental Resilience in Training 53
First Aid and Emergency Medical Considerations 54
Winter-Specific Medical Issues and Preparedness...................55
Building a Wilderness-Specific First Aid Kit 56
Staying Mentally and Physically Prepared for First Aid Emergencies 57
Safety and Risk Management Practices for Solo Travelers 58
Cooking and Nutrition in Cold Weather 61
Example: Winter Camping Meal Plan 63

Chapter 8: Leave No Trace – Caring for the Quiet Season 67
The Art of Campfires Without a Trace..67
Waste Management in Winter..69
Handling Waste Without a Trace 69
Cooking and Cleaning With Care 70
Embracing Silence and Solitude 71
The Power of Intention 71

Chapter 9: Creating a Base of Comfort and Security 73
The Comforts of a Truck Camper...73
Finding the Perfect Campsite...74
Creating a Drying Area Inside the Camper.................................75
Cooking Outside to Keep the Camper Fresh 75
Winter Camping in a Tent: Finding Comfort in the Ruggedness 76
Setting Up Your Tent on Snow 76
Layering for Warmth Inside the Tent...................................77
Final Thoughts: Respecting the Landscape and Preparing for the Unexpected..77

Chapter 10: The Road Ahead – Embracing Winter's Call 79
Why Winter?..79
Reflecting on the Journey 80
Evaluating and Replenishing Gear 81
A Backpack Ready for the Next Trip 82
The Cycle of Preparation and Experience 83
Looking Forward 83

Appendices: Various Checklists for Winter Travel 85
    Appendix A: Home Preparation Checklist for
    Extended Absence 86
    Appendix B: Must-Have Items Checklist for
    Boondocking Trips 90
    Appendix C: Detail Checklist for Winter Road Trip 92
    Appendix D: Essential Technologies for Backcountry
    and Boondocking Adventures 96
    Appendix E: Comprehensive Wilderness First-Aid Kit
    for Winter Adventures 100
    Appendix F: Apps Used for Planning, Determining
    Campsites, Navigation, Monitoring Technology,
    and Ski Mountaineering 106

About the Author 113

Introduction: The Beauty of Winter

"Winter's magic isn't in what it gives—it's in what it reveals: strength you didn't know you had and a world you might have overlooked."
—Thom Barrett

Winter camping and boondocking aren't for everyone. They demand a tolerance for cold, a strong sense of adventure, and a serious commitment to preparation. But for those of us who are drawn to the quiet beauty of the frozen wilderness, winter offers something truly unique. There's a stillness, a clarity to the world when it's blanketed in snow. The cold brings a sharpness to the air, and the landscape, stripped of summer's comforts, reveals its raw, elemental self. The solitude is profound, the silence complete—save for the crunch of snow underfoot or the distant call of a raven.

Winter is my favorite time to head out and explore, not just because of the beauty but because of what winter travel demands of me. It's a season that requires resilience, humility, and careful planning. There's a thrill in the challenge of exploring remote places entirely off the grid, surrounded by untouched landscapes that few ever see. In winter, every journey feels like an accomplishment, and every moment of warmth and shelter is hard-earned.

Over the years, I've come to recognize that there are different types of journeys we take into the wild, each with its own purpose, challenges, and rewards. These categories—adventure trips, sacred journeys, and expeditions—may overlap at times, but each one invites a different approach and state of mind. Understanding these distinctions has helped me prepare for my winter travels in a way that's both practical and meaningful.

Adventure Trips

Adventure trips are about seeking thrills, embracing challenges, and immersing ourselves in rugged environments. They're fueled by curiosity and a desire to test our limits. For me, an adventure trip might mean snowshoeing up a mountain trail to catch a view of a frozen valley at dawn or skiing across a frozen lake with no set destination in mind, just the promise of open space and quiet.

Adventure trips push us out of our comfort zones. They're unpredictable and exhilarating, demanding that we adapt to the landscape and weather, trusting our instincts and the preparations we've made. Winter amplifies this sense of adventure—the cold, the snow, and the isolation all add layers of complexity and risk. But with that risk comes reward. The feeling of accomplishment that follows a successful winter adventure, the memory of standing alone on a snow-covered ridge with the world stretched out below—it's something that stays with you long after you've left the wilderness behind.

Sacred Journeys

Sacred journeys are different. They're not necessarily about adrenaline or challenge but about a deeper, more personal connection with nature. These trips are about solitude, reflection, and reverence for the natural world. For me, winter is the perfect season for these journeys. The stark, stripped-down landscape mirrors a kind of inner simplicity, a quieting of the mind that's hard to find in busier seasons. In winter, the landscape is bare and honest. Everything unnecessary has fallen away, leaving only what is essential.

On a sacred journey, I might find myself drawn to a quiet forest clearing or a frozen lake at dawn. The goal is not to cover miles or reach a peak but simply to *be* in the landscape and experience the deep stillness that winter brings. These journeys remind me of my place in the natural world, of the smallness of human concerns in the face of something vast and ancient. There's a peace that comes from this kind of travel, a sense of clarity and renewal that's hard to find anywhere else.

For sacred journeys, my gear and supplies are minimal. I focus on staying warm, comfortable, and safe, but I don't burden myself with unnecessary items. I leave space for the experience itself to fill me, for the landscape to shape the journey, rather than my own expectations or goals.

Expeditions

Expeditions are something else entirely. They're about purpose, planning, and perseverance. An expedition is a journey with a clear objective—a destination, a summit, a specific challenge. These trips require intense preparation, as well as the resilience to deal with unexpected obstacles. Expeditions are often long, grueling, and mentally demanding. They're about endurance, and the satisfaction comes from achieving a goal you've worked for, often against difficult odds.

Winter expeditions, in particular, are not for the faint-hearted. They require a deeper level of preparation and caution, as the stakes are higher. In winter, a minor mistake can become life-threatening, so every detail matters. On an expedition, I double-check every piece of gear and every contingency plan. I bring extra food, additional layers, and redundant navigation tools. Expeditions require me to trust my gear, my preparation, and my judgment, and there's little room for error.

But the rewards are unique. When you reach the summit of a snow-covered mountain or complete a multi-day winter trek through the wilderness, you carry a sense of accomplishment that's hard to match. You've faced the elements, tested your limits, and proven something to yourself. Winter expeditions leave a deep sense of satisfaction because they demand so much. And what they give in return is the knowledge that you can survive and even thrive in one of the most challenging environments on Earth.

The Call of Winter

For me, each of these types of trips—adventure, sacred, and expedition—has its own place and purpose. Some journeys are about pushing myself, others about finding peace, and still others about achieving a specific goal. Winter offers the perfect backdrop for all three. It's a season that strips everything down to essentials, quiets the world, and focuses the mind.

This book isn't just a checklist of gear and supplies—it's a guide to embracing winter's demands and rewards. Every chapter is dedicated to one aspect of preparation, from securing your home to outfitting your vehicle, from selecting the best camping and survival gear to choosing the "toys" that make winter fun. It's based on my own experiences and the lessons I've learned along the way, from successes and mistakes alike.

If you're like me, winter boondocking isn't just an activity; it's a way of connecting with nature in its most powerful and beautiful form. Whether you're seeking the thrill of adventure, the peace of solitude, or the satisfaction of completing a challenging expedition, winter has something to offer. And with the proper preparation, you can experience it safely, comfortably, and fully.

So let's get started.

Chapter 1

The Last Look Back – Preparing the Home

> *"Survival begins long before you set foot in the snow. Preparation is your strongest shelter, and knowledge is your most reliable tool."*
> —**Thom Barrett**

Before I can focus on the road and wilderness ahead, I have to make sure the home I'm leaving behind is ready to weather the winter without me. Cold temperatures, snow, and ice can cause serious problems if I don't take the proper precautions. I've learned that if I want peace of mind while I'm out there, I need to know my home is secure, safe from the elements, and free of issues that could escalate while I'm gone.

Securing the Home

The first step is security. Even though I live in a quiet area, an unoccupied home can attract unwanted attention. A secure home isn't just about locks and cameras—it's about creating layers of protection and alerts that allow me to stay informed and take action, even from miles away.

For home security systems, there are plenty of options. Some systems simply capture video footage, letting me review it whenever I want. They're helpful for keeping an eye on things but require me to actively monitor the system. Others go a step further by offering professional monitoring services—these systems connect me to a team of support staff who are notified if an alarm is triggered. In case of a break-in or emergency, the monitoring team can take action on my behalf, alerting local authorities or contacting me as needed. This is especially useful for someone who's going to be off-grid or out of cell range for extended periods.

For my winter trips, I've opted for a combination of both video surveillance and real-time alerts. My cameras are set up to allow remote viewing, and I make sure the batteries are fully charged or connected to reliable power. Knowing I can check in on my home at any time offers a great sense of control, even when I'm miles away. I also installed various sensors throughout the house—motion detectors, freeze sensors, and flood sensors—that send alerts to my phone if there's unusual activity.

The freeze sensors, for example, are programmed to notify me if the temperature drops below 55°F, which could signal a heating issue and the risk of frozen pipes. The flood sensors are located in the basement and under sinks, and they are ready to alert me if any unexpected water leaks occur. These extra layers of security allow me to be proactive rather than reactive about potential home hazards.

Besides these digital safeguards, I take a few other practical steps. I double-check every lock on doors and windows, activate my alarm system, and set up motion-detecting lights around the front and back doors. To add an extra layer of human oversight, I let a trusted neighbor know about my trip, give them a key, and leave emergency contact information with them. That way, if anything goes wrong, there's someone local who can step in. Do not forget, though, to leave not only the key but also the code to turn off the alarm after they enter. I have not done this a few times and almost lost my neighbor because he was so alarmed (pun intended) that he almost had a heart attack.

Managing Utilities

Next, I focus on managing my utilities to prevent winter damage and reduce unnecessary energy use. I set my thermostat to around 55°F—low enough to save energy but high enough to keep the pipes from freezing. This single adjustment helps prevent what could be a costly repair if temperatures drop too low. As a backup, I have those freeze sensors to alert me if there's any malfunction with the heating.

I also turn off the main water supply before I leave. This small step protects my home from potential leaks or flooding, which can become disastrous if they go undetected for weeks. In addition, I unplug any non-essential electronics to reduce the risk of electrical fires and lower my energy bill while I'm gone.

The sensors I've installed also play a significant role here. If the heat drops or a leak occurs, I receive a notification, allowing me to arrange for someone to check on the house immediately. These small actions and devices add layers of reassurance, making sure that my home will stay safe and stable while I'm away.

Preparing for Weather

Winter weather is unpredictable, and snowstorms can happen with little warning. To prepare my home for the possibility of heavy snow or ice, I start with a few basics: cleaning out my gutters to prevent ice dams, inspecting the roof for weak spots, and making sure all exterior vents are clear. I also arrange for someone to clear my driveway if it snows heavily while I'm gone; an impassable driveway can make it harder for anyone to check in on the house or for emergency responders to access the property if needed.

Besides these steps, I make sure my generator is well-maintained, tested, and ready to kick in if the power goes out. Living in a wooded area prone to snowstorms and hurricanes means power outages aren't just inconvenient—they can also lead to serious problems like frozen pipes and spoiled food. A reliable generator provides an essential backup, keeping critical systems like heating and refrigeration running even if heavy snow or ice brings down power lines. Before I leave, I have the generator serviced and test it to ensure it's functioning correctly. This way, I know it's ready to take over if needed, sparing me the worry of unexpected power loss.

I also trim any tree branches near the house that could snap under the weight of ice or snow and cause damage. A heavy branch crashing down on a roof or window can lead to leaks, cold drafts, and even structural issues.

With these steps taken care of, I can head out on my winter adventure, knowing my home is prepared for whatever the season brings. By investing in security systems, ensuring a dependable power backup, carefully managing utilities, and protecting my property against winter storms, I've created a stable environment that won't demand my attention while I'm away. That peace of mind allows me to focus on the journey ahead—on the quiet, untouched landscapes and the freedom of the winter wilderness.

Chapter 2

Machines and Ice – Equipping the Vehicle

> *"In winter travel, the best companion is not courage—it's preparation. Your vehicle is your lifeline, and its strength is your safety."*
> —**Thom Barrett**

Out in the wilderness, my vehicle is more than just transportation—it's my mobile base, my lifeline, and even my shelter. A breakdown in the middle of nowhere isn't just inconvenient; it's dangerous. That's why, before any winter expedition, I have my mechanic do a full, bumper-to-bumper inspection. This review covers every critical system, ensuring that my truck is in peak condition to handle the extreme demands of winter travel with a camper in tow. This usually ends up costing me a few bucks, but in the end, the peace of mind goes without saying. If you are more adept at the mechanical side of things, the following may be helpful in what to review.

Bumper-to-Bumper Review of Both the Truck and the Jeep I Tow

My mechanic starts with a **battery health check**, testing the battery's charge capacity and load handling to ensure it can hold power in freezing temperatures. He also checks for corrosion on the terminals, cleaning them if necessary to prevent unexpected power loss.

One winter, I learned the hard way just how crucial a strong, reliable battery setup is. I woke up to find the camper batteries dead in sub-zero temperatures, miles from anywhere. These batteries were brand new, installed specifically for this trip, and rated for cold weather. On the recommendation of an "expert," I opted for two 6-volt batteries with longer amp life. The theory was sound: in some setups, 6-volt batteries paired together can provide more capacity than a single 12-volt battery.

What I didn't realize, though, was that many critical systems in my camper required a steady 12 volts to operate correctly. Anything less, and those systems simply stopped working. One such example was the power jacks I used to stabilize the camper for boondocking. Without enough voltage, I couldn't raise the jacks, which made it impossible to drive away.

Even well-insulated batteries take a hit in extreme cold. But with only 6 volts in each battery, if either one dropped below its rated voltage, I was in trouble—which I was several times on that trip. Thankfully, the redundancy of the batteries in the truck itself allowed me to recharge the camper batteries enough to limp through, but it was a frustrating experience.

It wasn't until I got home and talked it over with some buddies that I realized the problem was the 6-volt setup. I swapped them out for two 12-volt batteries, and I haven't had the same issue since. Now, battery testing and maintenance are non-negotiable parts of my pre-trip checklist. Knowing both the truck and camper batteries are up to the challenge gives me the confidence to start my day, even on those bitterly cold mornings.

With winter conditions in mind, he also inspects all **fluid levels and conditions**: using winter-grade oil for better flow in cold weather, topping up the transmission fluid, and ensuring brake fluid is fresh and moisture-free to prevent freezing. Antifreeze is verified to have the optimal mix for winter, and I use windshield washer fluid with anti-freeze properties to keep visibility clear on icy days.

The **brakes** are another area that receives close attention, as stopping power is critical, especially with a heavy camper load. I've equipped my truck with heavy-duty brakes designed to handle high temperatures and added strain—essential for safe descents down steep, icy roads. My mechanic checks the brake pads, rotors, and lines for any wear and tear, making sure everything is in perfect working order before I hit the road. Anyone who has traveled the Teton Pass can relate to the importance of good brakes. It has one of the steepest sustained grades in the region, reaching up to 10 percent. This requires a high level of driving confidence, and for me, it's a white-knuckle experience in snowy weather. Knowing that my brakes are not just in good working order but are heavy-duty with plenty of pads left makes a huge difference.

For traction, I've invested in dedicated **winter tires**—either Bridgestone Blizzak DM-V2, Michelin X-Ice Snow SUV, or Goodyear Ultra Grip WRT LT, depending on availability. These tires provide a superior grip on snow and ice, giving me greater control in challenging conditions. I inspect tread depth, look for signs of wear, and ensure the spare tire is ready to go, along with a tire repair kit, in case of emergencies. I would recommend checking the lug nuts after the tires have been installed. Having had my lug nuts sheared off while driving the plains of Manitoba because they were not torqued correctly was a lesson that could have ended up a lot more fatal than just losing a weekend in trying to get both back tires remedied. One actually came off as I was driving. I noticed this bouncing tire speed past me just before this loud crashing sound and jarring to the entire rig. It was an experience I hope no one else has to go through. Checking lug nuts is now a regular routine I have added during my morning walk around the rig before heading out for a day of travel.

The **heating and defrosting system** is also tested thoroughly. Clear windows are essential for safety, so I make sure the heater, defroster, and defogger are all functioning well. My mechanic checks the coolant levels and overall system performance to ensure the cabin stays warm and windows remain fog-free, even on the coldest days.

Visibility is crucial, so I replace my windshield wipers with **winter-grade blades** for better clearing in snow and ice. I also do a full check on all **lights**—headlights, brake lights, fog lights, and turn signals—to ensure maximum visibility for myself and others in low-light, snowy conditions. Fog lights do not get enough attention. In winter, during white-out conditions, they are huge in helping navigate the road.

Given the camper's added weight, I've taken extra measures to reinforce my truck's **suspension and steering**. I installed additional leaf springs, air shocks, and a heavy-duty suspension system, giving the truck a stable ride even with the camper load. This setup is essential for absorbing bumps and maintaining stability on uneven winter roads. My mechanic checks for any worn or loose components in the suspension and steering, as these are critical for control and safety, especially on snowy or icy terrain.

Belts and hoses also get special attention, as cold temperatures can make rubber components brittle and prone to failure. We inspect them all for cracks, wear, and leaks, replacing any damaged parts to prevent unexpected breakdowns. Similarly, the **exhaust system** is checked for leaks, as exhaust gases can accumulate dangerously if the truck becomes stuck in deep snow. We also make sure the tailpipe is clear of debris to avoid any potential buildup of carbon monoxide.

Finally, we test the **4WD system** to ensure it engages smoothly. In mountain driving, where extra traction is essential on icy or snowy roads, reliable 4WD performance can be the difference between moving forward or getting stuck. We also take care of my truck's locking hubs if they need adjustment.

These heavy-duty upgrades and checks are all part of my winter-ready setup. From additional leaf springs and air shocks to heavy-duty brakes and reinforced suspension, my truck is built to handle the added weight and stress of winter travel with a camper. With these preparations complete, I know I have a stable, reliable base to support my adventures in even the most challenging winter conditions.

Cold Weather Tire Pressure Management

Tire pressure can drop significantly in extreme cold, affecting traction and safety. I keep a portable air compressor in the truck so I can check and adjust the tire pressure throughout the trip, as colder temperatures can cause tires to deflate quickly. Monitoring tire pressure closely has saved me from slipping on icy roads more than once.

Early on, I didn't realize just how much the cold affected tire pressure. One winter, I was slipping around on icy roads, unable to figure out why my tires felt so unreliable—until I finally checked the pressure. It was dangerously low. Now, checking tire pressure is part of my daily routine, and it's saved me from some close calls on slick, winding roads. It's an easy process, too, thanks to the tire pressure gauges that allow me to monitor each tire from the comfort of the driver's seat.

Routine Checks and Maintenance Schedule

Routine checks are critical to prevent minor issues from becoming major problems in the cold. Every day, I habitually check fluid levels, tire pressure, battery charge, propane levels, and fuel supply. Winter conditions can quickly wear on these systems, so staying proactive with maintenance is critical. I also monitor the weather closely—using my Garmin inReach for satellite forecasts—so I can adjust my plans based on what's coming.

One lesson I've learned over the years is always to keep the gas tank at least half-full. This prevents gas line freeze-ups, which could otherwise leave me stranded in sub-zero temperatures—a scenario I'm not interested in testing. I've also installed a block heater to keep the engine warm during extremely cold nights. With the block heater plugged in, I can be sure the engine will start smoothly, even after a night of deep winter chill. This small investment has proven invaluable for cold starts when the temperature plummets.

Water Management in Freezing Conditions

Because water systems in campers aren't designed to handle prolonged freezing temperatures, I've made a conscious choice not to use the built-in water system during winter trips. I don't run water through the pipes, which means I don't have hot water from the tap. Instead, I bring along drinking water in separate containers and use snow as my main source of water for everything else. Each day, I melt snow and boil it to use for washing dishes, basic cleaning, and any other non-drinking needs.

Melting snow for water can be time-consuming, so I try to make it as efficient as possible. Sometimes, I leave containers of snow outside in the sun to pre-melt before boiling, or I use dark-colored containers that absorb sunlight faster. For storage, I keep my water containers insulated or inside the camper overnight to prevent them from freezing solid. These strategies help me conserve the drinking water I bring along and avoid issues with frozen pipes.

Ventilation, Safety, and CO/Propane Detection

Ventilation is crucial for staying safe and comfortable in the camper, especially when using propane for heat. I keep a vent slightly open in the bathroom for a few reasons (some of them obvious, haha), but mainly to manage moisture and ensure adequate airflow. This small opening helps reduce condensation, which is a constant battle in cold weather. Without ventilation, condensation can build up inside the camper, leading to dampness and even mold over time—not to mention the risk of carbon monoxide buildup when using a propane heater.

Safety is a top priority, so I've installed a combined CO and propane detector in the camper. This detector is essential, especially at night when I'm sleeping and might not notice any issues. Carbon monoxide is colorless, odorless, and deadly, and propane leaks can also be dangerous if undetected. My goal is simple: to wake up every morning safe and sound, and the detector gives me the peace of mind that I'll be alerted if something goes wrong with the propane heater or any other gas appliance. It's a small device but a vital part of my setup, helping ensure that I stay safe even in the most remote conditions.

Portable Propane Heater for Backup Heat

While my primary heater runs off the main propane system, I also carry a small, portable propane heater as a backup. This little heater has saved my butt on too many occasions to count. When temperatures drop especially low, the primary heating system can struggle to keep up, or I might run into issues with propane delivery at high altitudes. In those cases, the portable heater is invaluable. It's compact, efficient, and reliable, giving me an extra layer of security to ensure I stay warm, even in extreme conditions.

On a trip through Alaska, my main heater gave out in the middle of a particularly frigid night. The temperature inside the camper dropped fast, but since I was snuggled in my -30°F sleeping bag, I hadn't realized just how cold it was—until I noticed my dog shivering, trying to get as close to me as possible. Thankfully, I had my trusty portable heater, and I was able to get it going right away. That little unit kept us warm enough to get through the night until I could fix the primary system in the morning. After that, I decided I'd never go anywhere without it.

Having this secondary heater also gives me peace of mind if I'm ever caught without my main propane supply—whether because of altitude, extreme cold, or simply running out. It's a straightforward but essential item to include.

Fire Safety Precautions

Given that I rely on propane for heat, fire safety is a significant consideration. I keep a small fire extinguisher within easy reach and make sure it's rated for propane and electrical fires. This little precaution adds peace of mind, knowing I can act quickly if there's ever an emergency.

Managing Propane in Cold and High-Altitude Conditions

As someone who relies on propane to keep the camper warm, I've learned a lot about its limitations in extreme conditions—especially at high altitudes. Propane struggles to work effectively above 7,000 feet in cold weather due to the combination of lower atmospheric pressure and reduced temperatures. At higher elevations, the air pressure is much lower, which reduces the vapor pressure of the propane in the tank. In simple terms, propane has a harder time transitioning from a liquid to a gas, which is necessary for combustion. This can result in a weaker flame or, sometimes, a failure to ignite altogether.

After a particularly frigid experience winter camping in British Columbia, where I woke up to a cold camper multiple mornings in a row, I found a solution that made a world of difference: a twin-stage regulator. This device, while not large or complicated, regulates propane pressure in two stages, which helps maintain a more consistent flow of gas even when environmental conditions fluctuate. The staged reduction process draws a bit of heat from the gas, which can help prevent the regulator from freezing up in cold weather—a common issue when single-stage regulators struggle in low temperatures.

The twin-stage regulator has been incredibly beneficial in high-altitude conditions. Improving pressure stability reduces the risk of flame-outs and weak output, which are often caused by pressure drops from the cold or lower atmospheric pressure. Since installing it, I've experienced more consistent heating performance in both extreme cold and high elevations. Now, if I wake up to a cold camper, it's usually because I've run out of propane—not because the system itself has failed.

To further support propane performance, I carry two canisters, so I'm never caught off guard if one runs low. For extended stays at altitude, I sometimes use a larger propane tank, as the additional volume can help maintain vapor pressure better. These combined strategies allow me to feel more secure about my heat source, even in harsh winter conditions.

Learning to Manage Power in Extreme Cold

I've discovered through experience that extreme cold can be brutal on both power and heat systems. It took me a few winters to realize that when temperatures hover below -10°F for days at a time, the camper's batteries and heating system can simply give out. More mornings than I can remember, I'd wake up to find the inside temperature hovering at a "toasty" 20°F. The camper's electrical and heat systems would be dead, and I'd have to start the truck, relying on both of its batteries to recharge the camper's batteries just to get things running again.

To remedy this, I installed a battery heater in the compartment housing my camper's batteries. This minor upgrade has made a world of difference; the heater keeps the batteries warm enough to retain their charge even in frigid conditions, so I no longer have to rely on the truck to jumpstart my systems each morning. Along with the heater, I've learned to prioritize essential devices when power is low and to budget my power usage on especially cold days.

Navigation, Recovery, and Spare Gear

Reliable navigation and recovery gear are critical in remote areas where cell service is sparse or nonexistent. My truck is equipped with OnStar GPS, which provides location data even when there's no cell signal. This feature has come to my rescue multiple times when I've found myself off the grid, deep in the woods, or up in the mountains, where traditional GPS apps lose signal.

However, I didn't always realize just how valuable this feature could be. For a while, I depended entirely on my cell-based GPS—until I spent two days lost in a remote section of the Northern Cascades. The roads were endless, crisscrossing through dense forest, but each one I took seemed to dead-end. I wasn't too worried at first; after all, I had my camper with me, no time commitments, and plenty of food. But as time went on, I knew I needed to find my way out.

By sheer luck, as I was flipping through the truck's radio and apps out of boredom, I stumbled across the Navigation Module. I still thought it was cell-based, but when I turned it on, there I was—right on the map, no longer lost. I felt a mix of relief and, admittedly, a bit of embarrassment for not realizing I had this capability all along. That experience was a turning point; now, I fully appreciate having OnStar and the peace of mind it provides.

OnStar also offers emergency assistance and roadside support, which can be a lifesaver if I encounter any unexpected issues far from help. Knowing I have access to accurate navigation and emergency communication—even when I'm beyond cell range—gives me the confidence to venture further off the beaten path.

Along with digital navigation, I carry a dedicated handheld GPS device, detailed physical maps, and a compass. I've learned that technology can fail, especially in extreme cold, so having analog backups is non-negotiable. I also bring a satellite communicator, specifically a Garmin inReach, which allows me to send text messages and signal for help if I'm truly off the grid.

For off-road boondocking, I pack a complete recovery kit: tow straps, traction pads, and a winch mounted on the front bumper. Snow and ice can make even a minor detour treacherous, so these tools are essential for getting myself out of tricky situations. My recovery kit also includes a sturdy shovel and an axe. The shovel is indispensable for clearing snow around the tires, while the axe helps me clear fallen branches or logs that block the trail—both of which I've encountered more than once in winter conditions.

Spare Tires and Repair Kit

One flat tire on a remote trail can change everything. That's why I carry not just one but two spare tires, along with a tire repair kit, a portable air compressor, and a jack. I've been caught out before without the tools I needed to fix a flat, and it's a mistake I won't make again. In the winter wilderness, self-sufficiency is more than a convenience; it's a form of survival.

Solar Power for Off-Grid Living

Power management is another crucial consideration, especially when I plan to set up camp for several days without draining the truck's batteries. To keep my camper self-sufficient, I've installed a 100Ah solar panel on the roof, connected to a pair of 12-volt batteries that power my camper's essentials. The solar panel is equipped with Bluetooth monitoring, allowing me to check its performance and track historical data on sunlight levels. This allows me to plan my stops strategically, aiming for locations that get enough sunlight to keep my batteries topped up. It's a smart setup that ensures I can keep my lights, fans, and small appliances running without tapping into my truck's primary power supply. During an extended stay in a remote valley, my solar setup kept my essentials running without draining the truck's battery. Without enough sunlight, I'd have had to ration my power use, but the solar panel kept me fully operational, allowing me to enjoy the peaceful isolation without worrying about energy.

With each piece of equipment carefully checked and stowed, I know my vehicle and camper are ready for the journey ahead. These preparations may seem extensive, but out there, each item is essential. They aren't just tools; they're the foundation of my safety and independence in the wilderness. And with my truck fully equipped—from the OnStar GPS to the battery heater, twin-stage regulator, CO/propane detector, solar panel, and that trusty portable propane heater—I can focus on the adventure, knowing I'm prepared.

Every trip teaches me something new, reinforcing just how much respect winter wilderness demands. Thoroughly preparing isn't just about safety—it's a ritual that reminds me of the privilege and responsibility of exploring these remote, frozen landscapes. Out there, self-reliance is more than a skill; it's a way of life.

Chapter 3

Off-Grid Essentials – Preparing for Boondocking

> *"Preparedness is freedom in the winter wild. The more you know and the better you plan, the farther you can safely go."*
> **—Thom Barrett**

Winter boondocking, with no facilities, no conveniences, and no one around for miles, demands a self-sufficient mindset. There's a thrill to being entirely on my own, but it comes with responsibilities. One winter in the Rockies, I was snowed in for three days with no one around for miles. It was breathtakingly peaceful, but every small task—keeping warm, cooking, even just clearing snow—felt more intense. It was a reminder that out there, being self-sufficient isn't just a luxury; it's essential. I need the right gear to stay warm, safe, and well-fed in the wilderness. For me, the ability to venture out into winter's quiet solitude is worth every bit of preparation.

Shelter and Insulation

For shelter, I rely on a slide-in camper that fits snugly into the bed of my truck. This compact yet comfortable setup provides all the amenities I need: heat, a stove, a sink, a sitting/dining area, a bathroom (yes, a functional one!), and, of course, a place for me and my dog, Dexter, to sleep. This camper keeps us warm and secure, but I know that even the best insulation can lose heat, especially through the over-cab area. That's why I also use a sleeping bag rated for sub-zero temperatures and a thermal sleeping pad, both of which provide extra layers of insulation and warmth.

One Christmas morning, I was in Banff, Alberta, where it was a biting -25°F outside. As dawn broke, the first rays of sunlight started cutting through the cold. Even with the heater running, I could feel the chill creeping through the over-cab area. Thankfully, I had my -30°F sleeping bag and thermal pad, and Dexter was wrapped up in her own cozy sleeping pad, snoring contentedly. Those extra layers kept us warm through the night despite the frigid temperatures. Experiences like that make me grateful for every bit of insulation I've added to my setup.

Along with the camper, I bring a four-season tent designed to withstand heavy snow and strong winds. This tent serves as an invaluable backup shelter against the elements, but when I'm boondocking for extended periods, it also doubles as my outdoor cooking space. Setting up a designated cooking tent keeps food odors away from our sleeping area and creates a safe, weather-protected spot to prepare meals.

Food and Water Supplies

Winter camping demands more energy, so I make sure to pack high-calorie, nutrient-dense foods that provide lasting fuel. My supplies include nuts, oatmeal, energy bars, and other easy-to-prepare options that won't freeze solid in cold temperatures. I bring a cooler to store perishables, which I insulate to keep them from freezing completely. I wrap my water containers in insulation to prevent them from turning into solid blocks of ice overnight.

Hydration is critical in winter, even though it's easy to overlook. The cold can mask thirst, and dehydration can sneak up on you quickly. To prepare, I pack ample water and bring a portable water purifier, which allows me to melt snow for drinking water if needed. Staying hydrated helps me maintain energy and focus in the cold, isolated environment.

Emergency and Safety Gear

When you're off the grid, safety gear is not just a precaution—it's essential. Out there, help isn't just a phone call away, so I need to be prepared to handle any issues that arise. I carry a fire extinguisher, an emergency beacon, and a comprehensive tool kit. These items aren't just for convenience; they could save my life.

Here's a breakdown of the emergency gear I rely on.

1. **Multi-Tool and Knife**
   A good-quality multi-tool is the backbone of my emergency kit. With a range of functions—knives, pliers, screwdrivers, and wire cutters—it's incredibly versatile. I've used it for everything from cutting rope to tightening screws on my camper. Once, the clasp on my camper door froze shut, and I used the knife blade on my multi-tool to chip away the ice. That multi-tool has come in handy more times than I can count—it's a lifesaver for quick fixes.
2. **Screwdrivers and Cordless Drill with Bits**
   I carry a set of screwdrivers in various sizes, both flathead and Phillips, along with a cordless drill and a bit set that covers an array of screw types. In winter, fasteners can work loose, and having a reliable screwdriver or drill can make a big difference. My bit set includes specialized bits, like Torx and hex, which are useful for equipment that requires specific screw types.
3. **Torque Wrench**
   One item I never leave home without is a torque wrench. I learned the hard way that improperly torqued lug nuts can shear off and cause a wheel to come loose, especially under the strain of off-road travel. Now, I make it a point to check the torque on my lug nuts regularly. The torque wrench ensures I

apply just the right amount of force, reducing the risk of over-tightening or under-tightening.

4. **Pliers and Adjustable Wrench**
Pliers, especially needle-nose and vice grips, are handy for gripping, bending, and manipulating metal parts. I also bring an adjustable wrench for dealing with bolts and nuts in various sizes. Together, these tools cover a lot of ground for quick fixes and adjustments, especially in cold conditions where dexterity might be limited.

5. **Socket Set**
A basic socket set covering both metric and imperial sizes helps with more complicated repairs. Whether it's tightening a loose bolt on the camper frame or adjusting parts under the hood, having a socket set can save the day. I keep this set organized and easily accessible in my tool kit.

6. **Hammer**
A small hammer might seem simple, but it's surprisingly versatile. I use it for minor repairs, breaking through ice if something is frozen shut, or even pounding in stakes for my tent. A hammer is one of those tools you don't realize you need until you're in a situation that calls for it.

7. **Ice Scraper and Snow Brush**
An ice scraper and snow brush are essential for maintaining visibility on winter roads. I make a habit of clearing snow and ice from my windows, mirrors, and lights before setting out. It's a small step that makes a big difference in safety.

8. **Jumper Cables and Portable Battery Pack**
Cold temperatures can be hard on batteries, so I carry a set of heavy-duty jumper cables and a portable battery pack. The jumper cables are useful for jump-starting the truck if the main battery struggles, while the portable battery pack can handle smaller devices and accessories, keeping me connected and safe.

9. **Tire Pressure Gauge**
Winter temperatures can cause tire pressure to fluctuate, so I keep a tire pressure gauge handy. Underinflated or overinflated

tires are not only dangerous, but they can also affect fuel efficiency and vehicle handling. This simple tool lets me make quick adjustments as needed.

10. **Tow Strap and Traction Pads:**
    In addition to my winch, I carry a tow strap and traction pads. The tow strap is invaluable for helping other vehicles—or my own if necessary—get out of a ditch or snowbank. Once, on a snowy mountain pass, I found myself stuck in a snowbank. The traction pads gave me just enough grip to crawl out. Since then, I've come to rely on these simple but effective tools—they're a must-have for any winter adventure.

11. **Duct Tape and Cable Ties**
    Duct tape and cable ties are the unsung heroes of any emergency kit. Duct tape can temporarily fix everything from a leaky hose to a cracked window, while cable ties are excellent for securing loose parts or managing cables. These inexpensive items can make quick fixes that buy me time until I can make a more permanent repair.

12. **Flashlight and Extra Batteries**
    Winter means shorter days, and if I need to work on the vehicle in low-light conditions, a reliable flashlight is essential. I also bring a headlamp for hands-free work and pack plenty of extra batteries. Once, I had to replace a fuse under the hood in the middle of a pitch-black night. My headlamp was a lifesaver—I can't imagine fumbling through that without decent lighting.

13. **Shovel and Axe**
    A compact, foldable shovel is a lifesaver for digging out of snow. Whether I need to clear snow from around the tires or dig a pathway to my campsite, the shovel is an essential part of my kit. I also carry an axe, which might seem unconventional but is actually one of my most-used tools. One snowy morning in Michigan's Upper Peninsula, I woke up to find the road completely blocked by a fallen branch. My axe allowed me to clear it in about 15 minutes; without it, I would have been stuck there.

14. **Gloves and Hand Cleaner**
    Finally, I keep a set of heavy-duty gloves in my emergency kit, along with some hand cleanser. Working with metal tools in freezing conditions without gloves isn't just uncomfortable—it's dangerous. Gloves protect my hands from the cold, while the hand cleanser ensures I can clean up after handling oil or other substances that might get on my hands during a repair.

Chapter 4

Layered for Survival – Dressing for Winter's Wrath

"Dressing for the cold isn't about warmth—it's about survival. Layers aren't just clothes; they're your armor against nature's extremes."
—**Thom Barrett**

The right clothing is as essential as the right shelter when it comes to winter camping. Winter weather can change rapidly, and dressing in layers is vital to staying comfortable and safe. Anyone who has embarked on a hiking trail in the dead of winter can relate. Those first miles, you think about how easy things are and that you are glad for the warmth of your clothes. But after some exertion, you find yourself sweating profusely and stopping to peel off the layers. As the sun sets, the cold creeps back in, and you can quickly adjust by throwing back on that layer or more. Being able to quickly take away or add layers without having to stop for long makes a tremendous difference. Experiences like that have taught me always to be prepared for the unexpected in winter weather.

Layering allows me to adapt to different activity levels and temperatures throughout the day. During the daytime, when I'm active—hiking, setting up camp, or gathering firewood—my body generates a lot of heat. In these moments, my clothing needs to manage moisture and allow some heat to escape. But as night falls and activity levels drop, my clothing strategy changes. Whether

I'm sitting by the campfire, cooking outside, or simply relaxing in my shelter, staying warm becomes all about retaining the heat my body has generated.

For nighttime, I always bring an extra-warm down layer—both pants and a jacket—to trap as much heat as possible when I'm less active. Down insulation is incredibly effective at keeping warmth in, making it perfect for those long, cold evenings around camp.

Here's how I approach each layer to ensure I'm prepared for both active days and inactive cold nights:

The Layering System

1. **Base Layer**
   The base layer sits closest to my skin and is designed to wick moisture away. I choose materials like synthetic fibers or merino wool for this layer, as they pull sweat away from my body and dry quickly. Keeping my skin dry is crucial because moisture can quickly turn cold in winter temperatures. This base layer is essential during the day when I'm moving and building up body heat. Once, I underestimated how much I'd sweat on a steep climb and didn't change out of my damp base layer afterward. The moment I stopped moving, that damp layer turned icy against my skin, making me shiver uncontrollably. Now, I'm meticulous about choosing base layers that wick moisture and dry quickly.
2. **Mid-Layer Insulation**
   The mid-layer provides warmth and is usually made of fleece or down. During the day, a fleece jacket and pants work well for trapping heat without causing me to overheat. However, for nighttime or low-activity periods, I upgrade to down pants and a down jacket to retain as much warmth as possible. Down is lightweight and highly insulating, making it ideal for times when I'm not generating heat from movement. I remember

stopping for lunch on a ridge in Washington State, where the wind was relentless. Even though I wasn't moving much, the fleece mid-layer kept me comfortable enough to enjoy the view and my meal without freezing. I've learned that having a warm mid-layer is the difference between a quick, uncomfortable break and a genuinely enjoyable rest.

3. **Outer Shell**
   The outer layer is all about protection from the elements. I rely on a waterproof and windproof shell jacket and pants to shield me from snow, rain, and icy winds. This layer is crucial in winter conditions, as staying dry is the first line of defense against the cold. A good shell also provides breathability, so it can release moisture from within without letting in external moisture. One evening, just outside of Leadville, I got caught in a snowstorm while collecting firewood. The wind was whipping snow sideways, and without my waterproof shell, I would have been soaked through in minutes. That experience taught me that a reliable shell is non-negotiable in winter—staying dry is the first line of defense against the cold.

4. **Accessories for Extremities**
   Winter camping can be brutal on exposed skin, especially on areas like the hands, feet, ears, and face. On one trip, I ignored the early signs of cold feet, figuring I'd warm up once I started moving again. But my feet just kept getting colder, and by the time I got back to camp, they were numb. I spent the next hour trying to thaw them out by the fire. Now, I never skimp on warm socks or insulated boots—I've learned that once my feet get cold, they're hard to warm up again. I always bring:
   - **Thermal socks** to keep my feet warm and dry. I bring extra pairs to change into at night, as dry socks can make a world of difference in comfort.
   - **Insulated gloves or mittens** to keep my hands warm. Mittens are generally warmer, but gloves provide better dexterity, so I bring both.

- o **A wool hat** that covers my ears, along with a **face mask or neck gaiter** to protect my face. The head and neck lose a lot of body heat, so keeping these areas warm is essential.
- o **Waterproof insulated boots** with good traction. Cold feet can ruin a day, and slippery ground can be dangerous, so I make sure my boots are up to the task.

Important Considerations for Winter Clothing

- **Layering Flexibility:** Layering is essential because it allows me to adjust my clothing to match my activity level and the changing temperature. If I overheat, I can remove a layer, and if I cool down, I can add one back.
- **Avoiding Cotton:** Cotton is a poor choice for winter as it absorbs moisture and dries slowly, making it dangerous in cold weather. Wet cotton can make you lose heat quickly, so I stick to synthetic or wool fabrics that dry fast.
- **Fit and Comfort:** Winter clothing should fit well but not be too tight. Tight layers can restrict blood circulation, which leads to cold hands and feet. A bit of looseness in each layer allows warm air to circulate and acts as additional insulation.
- **Bringing Extra Items:** I always bring spare socks and gloves. These items can become damp during the day, so having a dry set for evening or sleeping is a morale booster. There's nothing quite like putting on a fresh, dry pair of socks after a long day in the snow.
- **Checking Weather Conditions:** Before heading out, I always check the forecast and adjust my clothing choices accordingly. Winter weather can range from mild to extreme, and preparing for expected conditions can mean the difference between comfort and hardship.

Staying Warm Around Camp

While I'm active during the day, I'm constantly generating heat, so my goal is to balance warmth and breathability. But when evening comes, and I settle down to cook or relax around the campfire, I switch to clothing that emphasizes warmth retention. This is when the down layers come out. A down jacket and pants allow me to retain body heat even when I'm sitting still. Around camp, my focus shifts from moisture management to heat retention, and down insulation is the best tool for that job.

I learned this lesson the hard way during a trip to *Rosie's Roost*, a remote A-frame shelter perched on Eagle Glacier in the Chugach Mountains. After a hard day's climb, my friends and I sat around the small table inside, talking over dinner. It's a minimalist structure—no heat, no plumbing, no power—just the basics for survival in the alpine. I was bundled up in multiple layers, but none of them were down, and I could feel the cold sinking into my bones. Meanwhile, my friend across the table looked perfectly cozy. When I asked him how he was staying so warm, he pointed to the down jacket and pants he was wearing. I made a mental note right then and there: as soon as I got back home, I'd be adding down layers to my winter wardrobe. And what a difference they make—now, even in the coldest evenings, I can sit outside and enjoy the solitude of winter without freezing.

For added warmth, I keep my extremities well-covered. Cold hands and feet are particularly difficult to warm up once they get chilled, so I make sure I have insulated gloves, extra-warm socks, and a hat that fully covers my ears. A neck gaiter or face mask is also essential, especially if there's any wind. Protecting my face and neck helps me retain heat and stay comfortable throughout the evening.

In the end, dressing for winter camping is about preparation and flexibility. By layering strategically and using the proper materials, I can stay warm and dry throughout the day, no matter what the weather throws at me. By switching to down insulation when the activity level drops, I ensure I can enjoy the quiet, still moments in camp without feeling the bite of the cold.

When I first started winter camping, I thought I could make do with my regular gear. But having the right clothing has transformed the experience—it's gone from a constant battle to stay warm to truly enjoying the stillness and beauty of winter. Now, I can focus on the adventure itself, knowing I'm prepared for whatever weather comes my way.

Chapter 5

The Real Fun – Gearing Up for Winter Adventures

> *"When you walk into the winter wild, you leave behind the noise of the world and step into a place where the only voices are wind, snow, and silence."*
> —**Thom Barrett**

All of this preparation isn't just for survival—I'm out there to embrace winter and enjoy the unique activities it offers. One early morning, I found myself snowshoeing through a grove of frost-covered trees, with sunlight filtering softly through the branches. The silence was absolute, except for the crunch of snow beneath my feet. I remember pausing, letting the quiet seep in, and feeling like I was the last person on earth. Moments like that are why I go to such lengths to be prepared—so I can fully enjoy the magic of winter without any worries.

With the right gear, winter becomes a playground, and I'm determined to make the most of it. From snowshoeing through quiet forests to skiing down powdery slopes, winter adventures require specialized equipment. Here's how I prepare for the different ways I engage with the season.

Snowshoes and Crampons

Snowshoes are essential for exploring deep snow without sinking, giving me the freedom to roam wherever I want. They're perfect for moving over snowy fields or trekking through wooded areas. If I'm hiking on compacted snow or icy trails, I add crampons or microspikes to my gear. These give me the grip I need to climb steep slopes and navigate frozen terrain safely. Snowshoes keep me moving on soft snow, while crampons provide stability on harder, slicker surfaces.

Skis and Snowboarding Gear

For areas with rolling hills and wide-open spaces, I love to pack my cross-country skis. Gliding over the snow is an incredible way to cover ground quickly, and there's a special magic in skiing through a silent winter forest. But when I want to explore steeper terrain or venture into the backcountry, I bring my alpine touring (AT) gear. This includes skis with skins for uphill traction, lightweight AT boots, and bindings that allow me to switch between uphill and downhill modes. I'll never forget the thrill of skiing down a powdery slope in the backcountry near Revelstoke. It was untouched snow, knee-deep, and perfect for gliding. But getting to the top was a challenge, and my AT gear—especially the skins—made it possible. Without that setup, there's no way I could have safely navigated both the ascent and descent.

My backcountry ski setup also includes a specialized backpack loaded with essential items. Safety is paramount in the backcountry, and the right gear makes all the difference. During a backcountry skiing course, we practiced using our avalanche beacons, probes, and shovels in a controlled environment. It was eye-opening to see how quickly snow can bury someone, even in a training scenario. That experience underscored how crucial it is to carry and know how to use avalanche safety gear. I hope I never have to use it, but I wouldn't step into avalanche-prone terrain without it.

Backcountry Ski Essentials

- **Avalanche Safety Gear**: This is the most critical part of my backcountry kit. It includes an avalanche beacon, a shovel, and a probe, which are essential for navigating avalanche terrain.

Knowing how to use these tools properly is just as important as carrying them.

- **Clothing Layers**: I pack extra layers to prepare for changing weather conditions, including a warm mid-layer (like a puffy jacket) and a waterproof shell jacket to protect against snow and wind.
- **Hydration and Nutrition**: Backcountry skiing requires a lot of energy, so I carry plenty of water and high-calorie snacks to stay fueled throughout the day.
- **Navigation Tools**: A map, compass, and the skills to use them are essential for finding my way back, especially if visibility changes or I go off the beaten path.
- **Repair Kit**: Small items like duct tape, ski straps, and a multi-tool are invaluable for fixing minor issues with my gear. I also bring a scraper to remove ice buildup from my skis and skins.

Additional Gear to Consider for Backcountry Skiing

Depending on the specific trip, I might also bring:

- **Ski skins** for climbing uphill on steeper terrain.
- **AT Crampons** for added traction on icy sections.
- **Goggles and sunglasses** to protect my eyes from sun glare and snow reflection.
- **Helmet** for head protection on steeper descents.
- **Hand warmers and foot warmers** for extra warmth in freezing conditions.
- **First aid kit** for treating minor injuries.
- **Snow study tools** (optional) like a snow saw, crystal card, and thermometer for advanced avalanche analysis.
- **Bivvy sack** for emergency shelter.
- **Wax** for both skis and skins to improve glide and prevent snow buildup.
- **Extra gloves** (light hiking gloves, insulated gloves, and mittens for extreme cold).
- **Headlamp** for unexpected delays after sunset.

When heading into avalanche-prone terrain, I never skip the essentials: beacon, shovel, and probe. They're the tools I hope I never have to use but wouldn't be caught without. A few years back, I heard about a group of skiers who got caught in an avalanche not far from where we'd been skiing the previous week. They survived, but only because they were equipped with beacons, shovels, and probes—and, most importantly, knew how to use them. That story has always stuck with me and reinforced my commitment to avalanche safety. Every few years, I make it a point to take an avalanche training course—it never hurts to work on these skills.

Snowmobile and Outer Gear

Sometimes, I'll rent a snowmobile to reach even deeper into the backcountry. A few winters ago, I rented a snowmobile to explore a remote valley near Kicking Horse. The speed and freedom were exhilarating, but the wind chill at 45 miles per hour was brutal. Even with a heavy, windproof jacket, I could feel the cold biting through. That experience taught me that snowmobiling in winter requires gear as tough as the terrain. Snowmobiling offers a different kind of thrill, allowing me to cover large distances quickly and access areas that would be challenging on foot or skis. But at 45 miles per hour, the cold can be intense, so I wear a heavier, insulated outer shell specifically designed to protect against high winds. This isn't just about warmth; it's about creating a barrier against the icy gusts that come with speed. A well-insulated, windproof jacket and pants are essential for keeping comfortable on a snowmobile.

Summary of Key Gear for Winter Adventures

1. **Winter Hiking and Snowshoeing**
    - Snowshoes: For exploring deep snow without sinking.
    - Crampons/Microspikes: For traction on icy or compacted trails.

2. **Backcountry Skiing Essentials**
   - Skis and Skins: Cross-country skis for flat terrain; AT skis with skins for climbing steep slopes.
   - Avalanche Gear: Beacon, shovel, and probe—non-negotiable in avalanche terrain.
   - Navigation and Safety Gear: Map, compass, headlamp, and a first aid kit.
   - Additional Layers: Puffy jacket, gloves, extra socks, and other cold-weather essentials.
3. **Snowmobiling Outerwear**
   - Insulated, Windproof Outer Shell: Heavy-duty jacket and pants to shield from wind and cold while moving at high speeds.
   - Eye Protection: Goggles or sunglasses to guard against sun and snow glare.

With all this gear, I'm prepared to embrace winter's challenges and opportunities. The snow, ice, and cold become part of the adventure, not obstacles to avoid. Every time I'm out there, whether snowshoeing through a quiet forest or skiing down a powdery slope, I'm reminded of why I embrace winter. There's a peacefulness, a kind of magic, that only comes in these cold, still places. The right gear allows me to experience that fully, turning winter's challenges into pure adventure. When properly outfitted, I can truly enjoy the unique activities winter has to offer, knowing I'm equipped for whatever the season throws my way.

Winter adventures are exhilarating, but they demand respect. Each time I head out, I'm reminded of the delicate balance between enjoying the wilderness and respecting its risks. My gear isn't just for comfort or convenience; it's what allows me to explore the backcountry with confidence, knowing I'm prepared for whatever challenges may come my way.

Chapter 6

The Mental Game – Preparing for the Journey Ahead

> *"The wilderness gives you no warning before it shifts. A sudden snowstorm or dropping temperature can turn a trek into a trial. Stay ready."*
> **—Thom Barrett**

Winter camping isn't just physically demanding; it's a mental game, too. The long nights, cold mornings, and solitude of the wilderness all require mental resilience and a high degree of caution. Preparation isn't just about packing the right gear—it's also about planning for the specific challenges of the area where I'm headed and understanding the risks of the landscape.

Do Your Homework: Research and Local Insight

Before I even start packing, I spend time researching the area I'll be exploring. Winter landscapes can be unpredictable, with conditions that change quickly and hazards that might not be obvious to someone unfamiliar with the terrain. Talking with locals is one of the best ways to prepare. People who live in or near the area often have valuable insights that go beyond what you'll find in guidebooks or online maps.

I make it a point to ask locals—whether they're rangers, guides, or experienced winter hikers—for advice about any problem areas, places to avoid because of unstable terrain, or spots with heightened avalanche risk. Often, they can look at the map I'm using and point out which trails or zones are best avoided in winter, saving me a lot of potential trouble. They may also have information on recent weather patterns, snowpack conditions, and even animal activity that might affect my plans.

If I'm venturing into avalanche-prone areas, local knowledge becomes even more critical. I want to know where recent slides have occurred and whether certain slopes are likely to become unstable in the current weather conditions. It's also helpful to understand the overall snowpack stability, which can vary significantly from one mountain range to another. Locals with avalanche training can offer guidance on current conditions, giving me a better sense of what I might encounter.

The Extra Caution of Solo Travel

Traveling alone in winter requires an extra layer of caution. Solo winter camping can be a deeply rewarding experience, offering solitude and a unique sense of connection with nature. But without a partner, the risks increase significantly. If something goes wrong—a fall, an equipment failure, a sudden change in weather—there's no one there to help. After a nice snowfall one evening, I was out snowshoeing alone in Rabbit Ears Pass when one of my poles suddenly snapped. It's a minor issue, maybe, but it drove home the point that every little piece of gear matters when you're solo. I had a spare in my pack, but that moment reminded me how crucial it is to be prepared for even minor setbacks when there's no one else around to lend a hand.

That's why I take every precaution I can. I plan my route carefully and share my itinerary with someone I trust. I make sure that person has detailed instructions on where I'll be, my expected timeline, and whom to contact if I don't check in. I also set specific times to update them on my progress whenever I have a signal or access to my satellite communicator. This way, if anything unexpected happens, someone knows where I am and can initiate a response.

Balancing Safety and Solitude

One of the main reasons I venture into the wilderness in winter is to experience true solitude. There's something deeply satisfying about being utterly alone in a snow-covered landscape, miles from anyone else. But with that solitude comes responsibility. Each decision I make must be weighed carefully, knowing that I don't have the safety net of a partner to rely on. On one trip, I was tempted to push on to a distant ridge just as a storm was moving in. But with no one to rely on if things went south, I decided to turn back. It was hard to give up on that goal, but knowing I'd made the safest choice brought me peace of mind. Out there, respecting the limits is as important as embracing the adventure.

That's why I prioritize thorough preparation, both mental and physical, for each trip. By combining solid research, local insights, and careful planning, I set myself up to handle the challenges of winter camping with confidence. Winter's beauty is a powerful draw, but it requires respect and vigilance. The balance between embracing solitude and prioritizing safety is delicate but essential.

Each winter trip teaches me something new—about patience, humility, or even the limits of my own strength. Last season, I learned to embrace the slow pace of winter camping, realizing that sometimes, the journey is more about presence than progress. The wilderness has a way of teaching you exactly what you need to know if you're willing to listen. The challenges of winter camping demand a strong mind, a flexible spirit, and a cautious respect for the landscape. It's not just about surviving—it's about thriving, finding peace in the stillness, and honoring the quiet power of nature at its most raw.

Building Mental Resilience

Once I'm out there, the mental aspect of winter camping takes center stage. The quiet can be both peaceful and challenging. One morning, I woke up to a world blanketed in fresh snow. The silence was overwhelming, as if the entire landscape was holding its breath. I felt a strange mix of peace and vulnerability, knowing that there was no one else around for miles. Moments like these remind me why I seek this kind of solitude—it forces me to be fully present in a way that's hard to find anywhere else. Winter landscapes are stark, stripped-down environments where the usual distractions fall away. I remind myself to be flexible and to embrace the pace of winter boondocking. Setbacks are inevitable—whether it's unexpected weather, gear malfunctions, or simply the physical toll of moving through snow and cold. Patience and adaptability are as important as any physical gear I bring.

I find it helpful to keep my mind engaged, so I bring a few things along for the slower moments: a book or two, my journal, and my camera. These small items help me stay grounded, offering a creative outlet or a way to unwind after a long day. On particularly long nights, I pull out my journal and jot down thoughts or sketches of the surrounding landscape. Writing helps me process the quiet in a way that feels grounding. One night, I spent an hour trying to capture the way the moonlight hit the snow-covered trees—just little details, but they bring a sense of purpose and connection to the solitude. There's a special kind of peace that comes with winter camping—a quiet, introspective calm that isn't about excitement or adrenaline. It's about connecting with nature in its rawest, most beautiful form and being fully present in the moment.

Mental Health and Mindset Tips for Long Stretches of Solitude

Winter solitude is a double-edged sword. On one hand, it offers a deep sense of peace and connection with nature that's hard to find anywhere else. The snow muffles sound, and the landscape becomes a blank canvas for your thoughts. But on the other hand, the isolation, combined with the cold, long, dark nights, can take a toll on your mental health if you're not prepared for it.

Whether you're out for days or weeks, maintaining a healthy mindset is as important as staying warm or having enough food. Here are some tips to help you stay grounded, positive, and engaged during extended stretches of winter solitude.

1. **Load Up on Books and Music**
    Before heading out, download plenty of reading material and music to your devices. You'll find that, in the quiet of the backcountry, getting lost in a good book is one of the best ways to escape the monotony that can sometimes creep in. If you're a Kindle Unlimited subscriber, you're in luck—download ten books before you set off, and if you find a rare pocket of cell service or Wi-Fi, you can switch them out for new ones.

    Music is another great companion. There's something comforting about having familiar songs to listen to when the night closes in, especially as you're tucked into your sleeping bag. A playlist you love can transform the mood, creating a sense of warmth and familiarity even in the most remote and frigid locations.

    A long time ago, I lived in Australia for a few years. At first, country music wasn't something I listened to. But after about six months, I felt a bit homesick, and for some reason, I decided to play *The Greatest Hits of Willie Nelson*. It was a way to feel connected to home, and somehow, it worked. Now, whenever I'm in a faraway place, I put on Willie, and it takes me right back to that time in Australia—a period I remember with great fondness. My first daughter was born there, and those memories always bring me a sense of comfort. That's the power of familiar music. It's a small ritual of comfort, a reminder of "home" that you can turn to whenever you need it.

2. **Establish Small Routines to Anchor Your Days**
   One challenge of extended solitude is the way time can feel strange. Without the usual cues from work, people, or schedules, days and nights blend together, which can make you feel adrift. Creating small daily routines can provide a sense of structure and purpose that helps keep you grounded. For example:
   - **Morning Ritual:** Start each day with something that feels intentional, like brewing a hot cup of coffee or tea and watching the sunrise. Taking a moment simply to breathe, be present, and express gratitude can set a positive tone for the day.
   - **Evening Wind-Down:** Similarly, create a small ritual before bed. This could be something as simple as jotting down a few thoughts in a journal or reflecting on the day. This nightly ritual can help you process any loneliness, fatigue, or anxiety, clearing your mind before sleep.

3. **Set Small, Achievable Goals**
   Setting small goals each day gives you a sense of purpose and accomplishment, no matter how isolated you are. Goals don't have to be big—they could be as simple as gathering extra firewood, hiking to a new viewpoint, or observing a particular tree or rock formation that caught your eye.

   One winter, I set myself the goal of carving something out of a piece of wood I found near my campsite. It was a tiny task, really, but each evening, I'd work on it a little more, refining the shape and smoothing the edges. By the end of the week, I'd carved a small model kayak, a reminder of the time I spend paddling in the warmer months. It was far from perfect, but now I have a collection of these wooden kayaks, each with its own story—about the wood, where I found it, and the solitude that shaped it. Each one has become a symbol of the time and patience I found in myself out there.

In winter, these goals might include tasks like efficiently setting up camp, preparing a specific meal, or observing changes in the landscape over time. Small, concrete goals give each day a sense of progress and can make you feel like you're moving forward, even when the environment is still and unchanging.

4. **Engage with Nature to Stay Present**
   One beauty of solitude is the chance to deepen your relationship with the natural world. Take time each day to be curious about your surroundings. Engaging with nature doesn't just keep you entertained; it also reminds you of the richness of your environment, which can be a powerful antidote to loneliness.
   - **Track Animal Signs:** Winter landscapes reveal animal tracks in the snow—fox, rabbit, deer, or even small birds. Spend a few minutes each day identifying tracks, noting how fresh they are, and imagining the lives of these creatures.
   - **Observe Snow Patterns and Weather:** The snow itself can tell stories. Notice how the patterns change over time with sun and wind, or watch the different ways snow accumulates on branches, rocks, and slopes. These observations help you stay in tune with your environment and feel connected to the landscape.

5. **Embrace Physical Movement as a Mood Booster**
   When you're camping in winter, movement isn't just about travel; it's also about staying warm and lifting your spirits. Regular physical activity releases endorphins, which help combat the mental fog that can settle in during long, cold evenings.
   - **Short Exploratory Walks:** Even if you're not covering ground, try to take a short walk every day. Wander around your camp, hike to a nearby viewpoint, or simply stretch your legs. Movement clears your mind, helps you stay warm, and makes the day feel structured.

- **Mindful Stretching and Breathing:** At the end of the day, try some gentle stretching in your tent. Focusing on your breath and releasing tension in your muscles is grounding and prepares you for rest. In the stillness of the night, this small act of self-care can make a huge difference in your mental well-being.

6. **Journal Your Thoughts and Observations**
   Bringing a journal is a small but powerful practice for maintaining mental health on solo trips. Writing your thoughts, worries, and reflections is like having a conversation with yourself. It's a chance to work through feelings of loneliness or fear, to remind yourself why you're out there, and to celebrate the small victories of each day.

   One evening, I was feeling particularly low—tired, cold, and questioning why I'd chosen to be out there alone. I sat down with my journal, and as I started writing, I found myself listing everything I'd seen that day: the tracks of a rabbit, the way the snow glistened in the morning light, the feeling of the wind on my face. By the time I finished, I felt calmer, more connected to the landscape, and more sure of myself. Over the years, this ritual has become a foundation for the books I've written. It's strange how one simple act can turn into something much bigger.

   You can also use your journal to track observations—what you notice in the landscape, changes in the weather, or memorable moments from each day. Over time, these reflections become a record of the journey and a source of strength. On more challenging days, reading back through your entries can remind you of your resilience and give you perspective.

7. **Practice Mindfulness and Gratitude**
   In winter solitude, it's easy to get caught up in challenges—staying warm, managing supplies, fighting off the isolation. When I first started bushwhacking and boondocking, mindful-

ness wasn't as accepted a concept as it is now. But I remember stopping often just to take things in. Whether it was a sunset that felt like it was painted just for me, a frozen waterfall that looked like a river of diamonds, or a vast, silent lake—after a while, it became a habit to pause, take a deep breath, and let the cold air fill my lungs. In these moments, I feel a profound sense of gratitude—for the solitude, for the surrounding beauty, for the stillness. It's as if the world has quieted so that I can be present.

But practicing mindfulness and gratitude can help balance this mindset, shifting your focus to the beauty around you.

- **Mindfulness in Nature:** Take a few moments each day simply to be still. Listen to the silence, feel the cold air, and notice the details of the landscape. Letting yourself be fully present in nature can create a profound sense of peace.
- **Gratitude Practice:** At the end of each day, reflect on one or two things you're grateful for. It might be something simple—the warmth of your sleeping bag, a hot meal, the glow of a sunset. Cultivating gratitude helps keep your spirits lifted and reminds you why you chose this adventure in the first place.

8. **Stay Connected—Even Remotely**

While you may be physically isolated, that doesn't mean you can't stay connected to others in spirit. If you have a satellite communicator or any way to send brief messages, consider checking in periodically with a friend or family member. Even a short message exchange can help combat loneliness and remind you of your ties to the world.

I often send one-liners to my daughters to let them know I'm still alive and kicking. One time, when I was lost in the North Cascades, their response came almost instantly: "You're doing amazing! Can't wait to hear all about it when you're back." It was such a simple thing, but in that moment, it felt like a lifeline—a reminder that I wasn't alone in spirit, even if I was hundreds of miles from anyone.

You might also bring along small reminders of loved ones—a photograph, a letter, or a trinket from home. These small connections to your everyday life can be a comfort in the quiet of the wilderness, grounding you and reminding you that you're not entirely alone.

9. **Embrace the Dark as Time for Reflection and Rest**
Winter nights are long, and it's tempting to feel restless when darkness falls early. But instead of resisting it, embrace this time for rest and introspection. The dark hours are an opportunity to slow down, reflect, and recharge. The long winter nights can feel endless, but I learned to appreciate them. One night, after a tiring day, I lay on my back in my sleeping bag, just listening to the quiet. In the dark, without the distraction of sight, my other senses seemed sharper—the sound of snow falling outside, the feel of my breath warming the air inside my camper. I realized that the darkness had its own kind of beauty, a space where I could let go of everything and just be.

Consider using these hours to write, listen to music, or enjoy the simple luxury of resting after a day of effort. Solitude allows you to slow down in a way that's rare in modern life—permit yourself to let go of productivity and allow the stillness to settle.

Final Thoughts on Winter Solitude

Out there in the winter wild, your mind can become both your best friend and your most formidable challenge. Quiet and solitude have a way of amplifying your thoughts, bringing clarity but also exposing you to the full range of human emotion. Through small routines, creative engagement with nature, and intentional moments of rest, you can cultivate a mindset that not only endures solitude but also finds beauty and strength in it.

Remember, the winter wilderness has its own rhythm, its own heartbeat. Embracing that rhythm and letting it shape your days is part of the journey. With a few thoughtful strategies, the solitude becomes less an obstacle and more a teacher, revealing parts of yourself that thrive in the quiet, untouched beauty of winter.

Chapter 7

Physical Conditioning and Health Preparation

> *"The weight you carry in winter is not just on your back—it's in your mind. Build your endurance, and you'll lighten the load."*
> **—Thom Barrett**

For winter backcountry travel, physical fitness isn't just a bonus—it's essential. On one of my first winter trips, I hadn't fully prepared for the physical demands of skiing through deep snow with a heavy pack. After only a couple of hours, my legs felt like lead, and each step was a struggle. It took everything I had to make the final mile. My legs were cramping, I'd run out of water, and with each step, the mental strain grew heavier, too. I couldn't help but wonder if I'd make it back. That experience taught me that winter travel requires a whole new level of conditioning—now, I never skip my pre-trip training.

The physical demands of navigating dense snow, carrying a heavy pack, and managing the cold can quickly drain your energy if you're not properly conditioned. Unlike a summer hike, where trails may be well-worn and the terrain predictable, winter backcountry travel often means you're creating your own path, especially after a fresh snowfall. Every step through dense, heavy snow requires stamina, strength, and mental resilience.

After that trip, I realized that winter backcountry travel isn't just an extension of summer hiking—it's a completely different beast. Now, when I prepare, I treat each training session as if I'm heading into that final mile again. I know that the endurance I build beforehand could make the difference between a manageable journey and a dangerous one.

The Realities of Winter Terrain: Blazing New Trails

Blazing a trail through untouched snow is a whole different experience than following a packed-down path. After a heavy dump of snow, the landscape transforms into a blank slate, with no footprints or clear markers to guide you. I'll never forget a solo trip where fresh snow had erased the trail completely. Without any markers to guide me, each step felt like a small act of faith, trusting that I was heading in the right direction. At one point, I thought I recognized a ridge, only to realize I'd veered off-course slightly. I had to stop, take a few breaths, and reorient myself with the compass. Blazing your own trail doesn't just test your legs; it keeps your mind on high alert, constantly assessing the snowpack, the slope, and the way forward.

If the snow is light and powdery (the kind some call "champagne snow"), it may offer less resistance, but in many winter conditions, it is dense and heavy. Walking through this kind of snow is like wading through knee-deep wet cement—it's exhausting and requires a high level of endurance.

Each step forward in deep snow demands more energy than you might expect. Lifting your legs higher to avoid dragging through the snow, stabilizing yourself on uneven terrain, and keeping a steady pace all contribute to fatigue. And when you're out there alone, every step requires focus; there's no one else to share the workload or encourage you to keep going. Preparing for this requires both mental and physical stamina, as well as the ability to pace yourself over long, demanding stretches of trail.

The Weight of a Pack Over Time

Carrying a fifty-pound pack might feel manageable when you first set out, but after hours of trudging through snow, that weight becomes a test of both physical and mental endurance. Every hour, every mile, the pack feels a little heavier. Muscles ache, shoulders burn, and the weight pulls you down with every step. If you're not prepared for this, the experience can quickly turn from challenging to overwhelming.

There is one trip in particular that stands out. We were doing a ski-mountaineering trip skiing from Vail to Aspen, staying at various 10th Mountain Division huts. I was the first one out after a heavy snowfall. The snow was knee-deep, and each step forward felt like a battle against gravity. After an hour of lifting my legs high just to make progress, my thighs were burning, and I was drenched in sweat despite the freezing temperature. In moments like that, you realize that winter travel is about pushing through resistance at every step. I remember hitting a point after several hours where the pack felt like it was pulling me down with every step. My shoulders were aching, my legs were on fire, and it was all I could do to keep my balance in the snow. I had to stop frequently to catch my breath and adjust the straps to redistribute the weight. When I finally reached the hut, I felt a mix of exhaustion and triumph. Dropping my pack was like shedding a layer of fatigue, but the journey taught me an important lesson: it's not just about having the strength to carry weight but the resilience to carry it through hours of challenging terrain. That experience taught me the importance of core and shoulder strength—it's not just about carrying weight; it's about carrying it through rugged terrain, as well as over hours, even when fatigue sets in.

Training to carry a heavy load over extended periods is crucial for winter backcountry travel. Strengthening your legs, core, shoulders, and back helps you manage the weight of the pack, while leg strength ensures you can keep pushing forward. Aerobic conditioning is also crucial, as a strong cardiovascular system allows you to sustain energy over long distances without wearing out too quickly. The stronger your body, the easier it becomes to manage the mental strain that comes with carrying a heavy pack for hours on end.

Building Mental Resilience Through Physical Training

There's a direct connection between physical endurance and mental resilience. When you're physically strong and well-conditioned, it's easier to stay calm, focused, and positive, even when fatigue sets in. But if your body isn't up to the demands of the trail, the mental challenges become much more difficult to manage. Winter backcountry travel requires you to remain level-headed, even when you're cold, tired, and alone. Fatigue can cloud your judgment and lead to mistakes, so conditioning yourself physically also helps prepare you mentally.

The endurance you develop through physical training isn't just about finishing a trail or reaching a destination—it's about having the mental strength to stay calm and make smart decisions, no matter how tired you are. When you've trained your body to handle the demands of winter travel, you're less likely to panic in difficult situations, allowing you to assess risks clearly, conserve energy, and take breaks when needed.

Pre-Trip Conditioning for Winter Backcountry Travel

Preparing for the physical demands of solo winter travel involves more than just general fitness. Specific exercises can help build the stamina, strength, and flexibility needed for carrying heavy loads, moving through deep snow, and staying injury-free in the cold. Doing practice hikes with a loaded pack was one of the most helpful parts of my training. I started with short hikes, gradually increasing the weight, and by the time I hit the trail for real, carrying fifty pounds felt second nature. I can't stress enough how much those practice hikes prepared me—not just physically but also mentally. Knowing I'd already carried that weight over similar terrain gave me the confidence to tackle longer, tougher days in the backcountry.

Here's a breakdown of the types of conditioning that are especially beneficial.

- **Aerobic Conditioning for Stamina:** Aerobic exercises like hiking, trail running, and cycling build cardiovascular endurance, which is essential for sustaining energy over long periods. In the winter, breathing cold air can be challenging, and a strong cardiovascular system helps you manage this better. Aim for long, steady sessions that mimic the pace and duration of a day on the trail.
- **Strength Training for Load-Bearing:** Winter travel with a heavy pack requires solid upper body and core strength, as well as powerful legs. Exercises like squats, lunges, deadlifts, and shoulder presses build the muscles that support load-bearing. Incorporating weight training helps your body adapt to the demands of carrying gear and shoveling snow, which will make everything feel more manageable in the backcountry.
- **Stability and Balance Exercises:** Moving through dense, uneven snow can throw off your balance and strain stabilizer muscles, especially in your ankles and knees. Adding stability exercises like single-leg deadlifts, step-ups, and balance board work can help improve your control over uneven terrain. This is particularly important if you're blazing your own trail in variable snow conditions.
- **Flexibility and Mobility Work:** Cold weather can stiffen muscles and reduce flexibility, increasing the risk of strain and injury. Incorporating flexibility exercises, like yoga or dynamic stretching, keeps muscles and joints limber. Mobility work helps you adapt to the physical challenges of snow travel, like lifting your legs higher than usual, bending down to adjust gear, or reaching awkwardly in your pack.
- **Endurance-Building Through Practice Hikes with Weight:** There's no substitute for practice when it comes to building

pack-carrying endurance. Before heading out on a winter trip, take several practice hikes with a fully loaded pack. Gradually increase the weight and distance to allow your body to adapt. This not only builds physical endurance but also gets you used to the specific demands of carrying gear in winter conditions.

Preparing for Trail-Breaking and Adapting to Heavy Snow

Even with physical conditioning, trail-breaking through deep snow requires an extra layer of mental toughness. The repetitive movement of lifting your legs through dense snow can be exhausting, and there's often no shortcut or easy way through. Learning to pace yourself is crucial—sometimes, that means slowing down to conserve energy, taking breaks to catch your breath, or even rotating routes slightly to avoid the deepest drifts. On one of my longer ski-mountaineering trips, we were ski-mountaineering from Chamonix to Zermatt; I was with a group of extremely experienced mountain climbers and ski mountaineers. One of them shared a tip with me, one that helped him when he climbed Mt. Everest. It's referred to as the "Everest Shuffle." It's a deliberate, energy-conserving method of walking that allows climbers to maintain steady progress in low-oxygen environments. This technique often incorporates the *rest step*, where climbers briefly lock their back leg with each step to transfer some of the load to their skeletal structure. This prevents muscle fatigue and helps maintain a sustainable pace.

The shuffle involves taking small, deliberate steps, almost like a slow, controlled glide. This minimizes energy expenditure and helps conserve oxygen. Combined, the Everest Shuffle and rest step allow climbers to move steadily and reduce the strain on their muscles and respiratory system in the thin air. I found this extremely helpful in maintaining energy over longer distances. Learning the Everest Shuffle completely changed the way I approached trail-breaking in heavy snow. By slowing down and focusing on conserving energy with each step, I found I could maintain a steady pace over much longer distances. In challenging conditions, it's often the small techniques that make the most significant difference.

Understanding that winter backcountry travel isn't "just a walk in the woods" sets the right mindset for the journey. In dense snow, a mile can feel like three, and a simple ascent can turn into a test of willpower. Knowing what to expect physically—and training accordingly—can be the difference between a successful adventure and one cut short by exhaustion or injury.

Building Mental Resilience in Training

One of the most valuable aspects of physical conditioning for winter travel is that it also builds mental resilience. Endurance activities naturally test your focus and perseverance, and you learn to push through discomfort in a controlled way. Training in this way prepares you not only to handle the physical challenges of winter travel but also to stay calm and positive when conditions get tough.

Conditioning your body to handle a heavy pack, dense snow, and the relentless demands of trail-breaking allows you to approach winter travel with a clear head and the confidence that you're physically prepared for the journey. When your body is strong, your mind can focus on the beauty and magic of the landscape rather than the strain of each step. By training well, you give yourself the freedom to fully experience the rewards of winter backcountry travel—on your terms, with confidence and resilience.

Now, when I'm out in the winter wilderness, I can focus on the landscape—the beauty of untouched snow, the quiet of the forest—instead of constantly fighting against physical strain. Training well gives me the freedom to be fully present, embracing the peace and magic of the journey with confidence and resilience.

First Aid and Emergency Medical Considerations

First aid is always an essential part of backcountry travel, but in winter settings, it takes on a heightened level of importance. The combination of extreme cold, remote locations, and limited response times can turn a minor injury or medical issue into a serious, potentially life-threatening situation. When you're traveling alone or far from help, a strong foundation in first aid and emergency response is as critical as any piece of equipment in your pack.

One of the best ways to prepare for these scenarios is by taking wilderness-specific medical courses. Programs offered by organizations like the National Outdoor Leadership School (NOLS), Wilderness Medicine Institute (WMI), and Stonehearth Open Learning Opportunities (SOLO) provide specialized training that goes beyond standard first aid. These courses, which are often offered in spring and fall, teach skills that can be invaluable in the winter wilderness, covering everything from hypothermia management to long-term care for injuries when rescue is delayed. A Wilderness First Aid (WFA) course is an excellent entry point, offering basic skills that help you handle common backcountry medical situations. For those venturing further into the wilderness or for extended periods, a Wilderness First Responder (WFR) course offers a deeper level of training, including protocols for assessing injuries, managing trauma, and stabilizing patients over long durations.

For those planning to travel in avalanche-prone areas, avalanche training is critical. Organizations like the American Institute for Avalanche Research and Education (AIARE) offer Avalanche Level 1 courses that teach you how to read snowpack, assess terrain, and identify red flags that indicate avalanche risk. This training is often combined with hands-on practice in using avalanche safety gear—beacons, shovels, and probes—which you should not only carry but know how to use proficiently. Many avalanche courses also cover what to do in the event of an avalanche burial, including organized search techniques and managing an avalanche victim's airway and breathing in snow.

For those interested in honing their survival skills, backcountry or survival courses offer training in navigation, shelter-building, and cold-weather survival techniques. These courses go beyond first aid to provide a broader skill set that's invaluable in the winter wilderness, from finding and purifying water to building fires in extreme conditions. By developing these skills, you increase your resilience in emergencies, especially if you're traveling solo or in very remote areas.

Beyond formal courses, it's also helpful to refresh your skills and knowledge periodically. Many people who have previously taken first aid or avalanche training benefit from an annual refresher, especially if it's been a while since their last course. Knowing how to respond to a medical emergency, assess environmental hazards, or navigate in low-visibility conditions requires more than just knowledge—it requires practice. By staying current with your training, you're better prepared to respond quickly and confidently in high-stress situations.

Winter-Specific Medical Issues and Preparedness

When packing for a winter trip, it's essential to understand the medical issues that are more common in cold environments. Hypothermia, frostbite, and cold-related injuries require specific care, and each one presents unique challenges in winter conditions.

- **Hypothermia:** Hypothermia occurs when the body loses heat faster than it can generate it, leading to a dangerous drop in core temperature. Symptoms can start subtly, with shivering and mild confusion, but escalate quickly to impaired judgment and loss of motor skills. In extreme cases, hypothermia can be fatal. Knowing how to recognize the early signs and treat them is essential. Treatments include providing warmth, using a thermal blanket, and removing any wet clothing.
- **Frostbite:** Frostbite is another serious risk in winter settings, especially for exposed skin on the hands, feet, nose, and ears. Early

signs include numbness and tingling, followed by a waxy, pale appearance. Severe frostbite can cause permanent tissue damage if not treated promptly. A good wilderness first aid kit should include supplies like sterile dressings to cover frostbite areas and chemical hand warmers to help prevent frostbite in the first place.
- **Sprains, Strains, and Fractures:** Snow and ice make backcountry travel inherently risky, and falls are common, especially on steep or slippery terrain. A wilderness-specific first aid kit should include splinting materials, elastic bandages, and trauma supplies to stabilize a sprain or fracture. Cold temperatures slow down blood flow and healing, so it's imperative to manage injuries carefully to prevent complications.
- **Dehydration and Altitude Sickness:** In winter, it's easy to forget to drink enough water, leading to dehydration. The dry winter air and physical exertion increase fluid loss, so carrying a water filter or purifier for melting snow is essential. For those traveling at high elevations, altitude sickness can be an additional risk. Symptoms include headaches, nausea, and fatigue, and the cold can exacerbate these symptoms. Knowing how to recognize and manage mild altitude sickness can be lifesaving.

Building a Wilderness-Specific First Aid Kit

Besides taking the right training courses, solo winter travelers should pack a wilderness-specific first aid kit. This kit goes beyond what you'd bring on a typical hike, covering a broader range of potential issues. Key items include:

- **Thermal Blanket or Bivvy Sack:** Essential for treating hypothermia and providing emergency shelter.
- **Blister Treatment Supplies:** Winter boots and snowshoes can cause blisters, which can quickly become painful and limiting. Carry moleskin, blister bandages, and antiseptic wipes.
- **Trauma Supplies:** Items like a tourniquet, clotting agents, wound dressings, and splinting materials are crucial for

managing severe injuries. Trauma supplies allow you to stabilize injuries and prevent further damage until help can arrive.

- **Chemical Hand Warmers:** These are useful for preventing frostbite and for keeping batteries and sensitive electronics warm in freezing temperatures.
- **Pain Relievers and Anti-Inflammatories**: Cold and physical exertion can cause joint pain and muscle soreness. Anti-inflammatory medications can help keep you moving if you're injured or dealing with discomfort.
- **Electrolyte Tablets:** These are useful for preventing dehydration, which can easily occur in cold conditions without regular hydration.

These items, combined with a solid foundation of wilderness first aid knowledge, prepare you for a range of potential scenarios. And while it may seem like over-preparation, remember that in the winter wilderness, minor issues can quickly escalate. The right equipment and knowledge can make all the difference, transforming an emergency into a manageable situation.

Staying Mentally and Physically Prepared for First Aid Emergencies

In a backcountry setting, preparation is as much mental as it is physical. Besides carrying a well-stocked first aid kit and knowing how to use each item, it's essential to be mentally ready to respond to an emergency alone. First aid and survival courses emphasize this mindset, encouraging participants to stay calm, assess situations thoroughly, and make clear-headed decisions even under stress.

Winter conditions demand a high level of preparedness and self-reliance, but they also reward those who respect their power. By equipping yourself with skills, knowledge, and the right tools, you're not only safeguarding your adventure but enriching it. Each course you take and every skill you learn contributes to your confidence in the backcountry, allowing you to experience winter's beauty without being at its mercy. For those who take the time to prepare, winter offers a world of quiet magic and discovery tempered with a profound sense of respect and readiness.

Safety and Risk Management Practices for Solo Travelers

There's a unique allure to solo winter travel—a solitude that brings you closer to the landscape and a quiet satisfaction in knowing you're entirely self-reliant. But this solitude also means higher stakes. Without a partner, every decision and every bit of preparation falls squarely on your shoulders. Traveling alone in the winter wilderness requires an elevated level of caution, planning, and awareness. Over the years, I've come to rely on a set of safety practices that help me stay prepared and, perhaps most importantly, adaptable.

The first essential practice is establishing a communication plan. Before I leave, I share my itinerary with a trusted contact—someone who knows the area I'm heading into and understands the significance of each check-in. I made the mistake of selecting someone who did not have this "sensitivity" and wasn't checking our communication channel regularly, primarily because they were in a different time zone. I don't just give them my start and end dates; I break down my expected route, stopping points, and estimated times for each significant milestone. We agree on specific check-in times so they know when to expect updates. If they don't hear from me within a specific window, they know exactly who to contact and what details to provide for a potential search. This isn't just about letting someone know where I am; it's a lifeline, a layer of accountability and security that ensures a response if something goes wrong.

For authentic remote travel, I carry a satellite communicator. In places where cell service fades out, these devices become indispensable. With a satellite communicator, I can send GPS coordinates and messages, and I have an SOS button that can alert emergency services directly. Before each trip, I pre-enter key contacts and draft standardized messages: "Doing well. On track," or "Setback, but in control"—to save time and ensure clarity, especially if I need to send updates quickly under stress. Staying connected—however loosely—is a comfort and an essential part of managing risk on a solo journey. I also make it a habit to test my communicator (in my case, inReach) just before heading off the grid. There's reassurance in knowing the device works and that my contacts are in place.

No matter how carefully I plan, I know winter conditions can change rapidly. That's why I always prepare "exit strategies." For every trip, I map out alternate routes in case my primary path becomes impassable. I also make a point of identifying any safety shelters or warming huts along the way. These can be lifesavers in extreme weather, offering a safe place to rest, warm up, or ride out a storm. Knowing where they're located gives me the security of a fallback option if conditions deteriorate. Solo travel means I have to be ready to turn back if conditions become unsafe, and having these contingency plans mapped out allows me to make those decisions without hesitation.

Packing for a solo winter trip means considering every potential scenario. I carry a bivvy sack or emergency shelter I can set up quickly if I find myself stranded. Even if I have a tent, the bivvy is there as an emergency backup—small, lightweight, and designed to provide critical insulation and protection from the wind. Hypothermia is a genuine risk, so I pack extra heat sources: chemical hand warmers, a reliable fire-starting kit with waterproof matches and firelighters, and sometimes even a small stove. Being able to generate heat in winter isn't just a comfort—it's a lifeline.

Then there's the first aid kit, which goes beyond the basics when I'm traveling solo. Besides bandages and antiseptics, I include trauma supplies like a tourniquet, clotting agents, and wound dressings, knowing that even minor injuries can become major complications when you're alone. And because having the supplies is only half the battle, I make sure I'm well-practiced in using each item. In the wilderness, especially in winter, wilderness first aid skills are invaluable.

Monitoring my physical and mental state is another crucial element of solo travel. In winter, moving through deep snow with a heavy pack is exhausting, and without a partner to share the load or encourage me when my energy wanes, I have to be hyper-aware of my limits. Pacing myself is crucial, as is recognizing when I need a break. Pushing myself too hard isn't just uncomfortable; it's dangerous, leading to mistakes in judgment and putting me at risk of injury. The cold and isolation can amplify feelings of fatigue or anxiety, so I check in with myself regularly, reminding myself that there's no shame in turning back if necessary. Solo travel is about endurance and resilience, not pushing boundaries recklessly.

Winter terrain is unforgiving, and understanding the environmental hazards is vital. In avalanche-prone areas, I take time to study the snowpack and read the landscape, assessing the conditions before committing to any route. My pack always includes an avalanche beacon, shovel, and probe. But carrying these tools isn't enough; I make sure I'm confident in using them. This is gear I hope I'll never need, but in winter backcountry, it's non-negotiable. Being aware of other snow hazards, like cornices or unstable slopes, adds another layer of vigilance, especially when I'm out there alone.

Navigation skills are another cornerstone of solo winter travel. While I rely on GPS, I don't depend on it exclusively. Cold weather drains batteries quickly, and technology has its limits, especially in extreme conditions. That's why I always carry a physical map, a compass, and waterproof markers. Before each trip, I take the time to mark my primary route, my exit routes, and potential shelters. These analog tools are a safety net, ensuring that if visibility drops or my GPS fails, I still have a way to find my path.

Staying mentally grounded is perhaps the most critical aspect of solo winter travel. Without a partner, it's easy to become overwhelmed by the silence, the cold, and the sheer remoteness of the landscape. I set achievable goals each day, aiming to reach specific points without overextending myself. I also establish a daily routine—setting up camp, checking my gear, and preparing meals. This structure brings a sense of normalcy and focus, and it helps me stay calm in an environment that can sometimes feel daunting.

Before every trip, I conduct a personal safety assessment. Am I physically fit enough for the terrain? Am I mentally prepared for the challenges of isolation and winter weather? Solo winter travel is not the place for ego or pushing untested limits; it's about respecting the wilderness and understanding my own boundaries. I review my emergency procedures and make sure I'm comfortable with every piece of gear, practicing with it at home if necessary. By preparing myself mentally and physically, I go into each trip with the confidence that I can handle whatever comes my way.

Solo winter travel is immensely rewarding, offering a rare connection to nature and a profound sense of independence. But it demands respect for the risks, meticulous planning, and a commitment to safety at every step. For those willing to embrace its challenges, it offers unparalleled beauty, peace, and self-discovery. And with the proper preparation and mindset, it's possible to experience that magic while minimizing the risks.

Cooking and Nutrition in Cold Weather

In winter's grip, cooking becomes a task of warmth, sustenance, and a small kind of ritual. The routines of summer camping fall away, replaced by new strategies and careful choices that keep you going in the cold. Out there, every meal has a purpose: to fuel, to heat, and to offer a touch of comfort against the chill.

Embracing The Cold

You start the day as the sun rises, pale and slow over the snow-covered landscape. Pulling on layers with stiff fingers, you're already grateful for the promise of a hot breakfast. In winter, you can't just grab a cold energy bar or a handful of trail mix to get moving; you need something substantial, something to wake you up from the inside out. You unpack a bag of oats, already pre-mixed with powdered milk, dried berries, nuts, and a pinch of cinnamon. This is where winter cooking gets practical—everything is measured out beforehand, ready to go, so you're not fumbling with loose ingredients in the cold.

As the oatmeal simmers, you add a dollop of coconut oil. In summer, you might skip this step, but in winter, that extra fat is a calorie-rich boost that will keep you warmer longer. Fat is slow-burning energy, and out there, it's your best friend. Each bite is warm, comforting, and nourishing, and the cinnamon-scented steam is a rare pleasure on a frigid morning. Breakfast isn't just fuel—it's a psychological lift, a moment of warmth before you step back into the elements.

You've learned that winter cooking starts with the right fuel for your stove. A typical butane canister might sputter in the cold, leaving you frustrated and hungry. So you've brought along an isobutane-propane blend, which performs better in low temperatures. You've also kept the canister close to your body all night, letting your body heat keep it from freezing. It's a minor trick, but in winter, minor tricks make all the difference.

By midday, you're halfway up a trail, and it's time for a quick, high-energy lunch. In winter, lunch is less about sitting down and more about grabbing calories and moving on. You pull out a wrap you prepared at camp—a tortilla filled with slices of hard cheese and salami, high in fat and protein to keep you going. The cheese hasn't frozen, thanks to being wrapped up in your clothing all morning. It's simple but effective: each bite is salty, savory, and energizing. And, just in case, you've packed a thermos of hot soup you made the night before, still warm thanks to the insulated container. Sipping the soup is like drinking warmth itself, a much-needed pause in the cold.

As the day wears on and your energy wanes, a few high-fat snacks become your lifeline. You pull out a handful of trail mix with nuts and chocolate, careful to eat it while it's still soft. Even something as simple as trail mix is different out there—if you don't keep it close to your body, it'll freeze solid by lunchtime. These snacks are pre-portioned, calorie-dense, and easy to reach in your pockets, providing little bursts of fuel as you move through the landscape.

By evening, you're ready for the heart of winter cooking: dinner. This meal isn't just about refueling—it's a way to close out the day and warm your body before sleep. You set up a small tarp as a cooking shelter away from your sleeping area. Even in winter, you respect the rule of separating food and sleep—no sense in tempting a curious bear, even if they're mostly hibernating. You start by boiling water, savoring the sound of it bubbling against the quiet night.

Tonight's dinner is a simple lentil stew, something you've made dozens of times but never grow tired of. The ingredients were pre-measured at home: a bag of dried lentils, some dehydrated vegetables, and a spice mix that fills the cold air with the scent of cumin and garlic as it simmers. This isn't just food—it's warmth, comfort, and familiarity. You drizzle in some olive oil for extra calories, watching it swirl through the stew, turning each spoonful into something rich and satisfying.

Example: Winter Camping Meal Plan

Day 1

Breakfast:
You wake to the chill and immediately reach for your pot and oatmeal bag filled with oats, powdered milk, nuts, and dried fruit. A quick

boil on the stove, a swirl of coconut oil, and you have a hot breakfast that fills you with warmth and energy. Each spoonful is creamy and satisfying, and the dried fruit adds just a hint of sweetness.

Lunch:
By midday, you're ready for something substantial but quick. From your pocket, you pull out a tortilla wrap you made that morning. It's stuffed with cheddar and salami, the perfect combination of fat and protein. You sit for a moment to enjoy it, the savory taste reminding you of simpler comforts. A sip of hot soup from your thermos keeps you going, a little pocket of warmth in the cold.

Dinner:
With darkness settling in, you hunker down to cook. Tonight's dinner is a hearty stew of lentils, quinoa, and dehydrated vegetables, seasoned with cumin and a bit of garlic. A splash of olive oil gives it a rich texture, and the entire meal feels like a reward for the day's efforts. You sit back, savoring the hot meal, letting the warmth spread through you as you reflect on the day.

Day 2

Breakfast:
Another cold morning, another hot bowl of oatmeal. This time, you add a spoonful of peanut butter for extra calories and protein. It's nutty, warm, and satisfying—a small but powerful start to the day.

Lunch:
Today, you opt for high-fat cheese and jerky, which are easy to eat on the go. The jerky provides a burst of salt, while the cheese offers slow-burning energy. It's not fancy, but it's effective, and it leaves you ready for the afternoon's hike.

Dinner:
Tonight's dinner is a quick couscous and vegetable medley cooked with ghee to add richness. The couscous cooks fast, saving fuel,

and the ghee provides both flavor and calories. You finish with a cup of hot chocolate, savoring the last warmth of the day as the temperature drops outside.

Winter demands meals that are both hearty and easy to make. You don't have the luxury of fresh ingredients or long cook times, so you rely on foods that are lightweight, filling, and nutrient-dense. And while you love the idea of cooking from scratch, you aren't above using dehydrated vegetables or grains when they save time and fuel. Each spoonful of stew feels like a small victory against the cold; each sip is a reminder that you're well-prepared, resilient, and comfortable out there in the wild.

Chapter 8

Leave No Trace – Caring for the Quiet Season

> *"Respect for the wilderness isn't just in how you tread—it's in how you leave it: untouched, unharmed, and unmarked by your passing."*
> **—Thom Barrett**

Winter is a season of extraordinary beauty and stillness—snow blankets the land, muffling sounds and transforming the landscape into something timeless and pristine. The backcountry in winter feels untouched, like a place outside of time, and that sense of purity invites us to tread lightly. But winter, with all its silence and starkness, is also a fragile season. The decisions we make—where we camp, how we cook, and what we leave behind—can leave an impact that will be visible long after the snow has melted.

The Leave No Trace principles guide us in this stewardship. They're not just about packing out our trash; they're about being mindful of how every action, no matter how small, shapes the land we leave behind.

The Art of Campfires Without a Trace

Few things feel as comforting on a winter night as a crackling campfire. The flickering light and warmth can feel like a small miracle in the cold. But a campfire, especially in winter, has the power to leave scars if we're not careful. Beneath the snow lies a delicate ecosystem; plants and soil are dormant and waiting for spring. A fire built directly on snow will melt down to the ground, burning the surface below and leaving a blackened ring of scarred earth.

One winter, while boondocking in Teton National Park, I had a fire going in my Solo Stove when a park ranger came sauntering up. I offered him a cup of hot coffee, and we started talking. He made a few positive comments about my rig and then got to the reason he'd stopped by. He'd seen the smoke and assumed I'd built a traditional fire on the ground, so he was ready to give me the standard Leave No Trace lecture on the impact of campfires. But when he saw that the fire was contained, controlled, and not affecting the ground, he accepted the coffee, and we chatted for a while. That encounter reminded me how important it is to take every step to minimize our impact—even a single fire can leave a lasting mark if it's not managed carefully.

There are ways, however, to enjoy a fire without leaving a trace. A fire pan is a portable metal container designed to hold a fire above ground level. Raising the flames prevents the heat from searing the earth below. Imagine a shallow metal tray with raised edges—sturdy enough to contain a fire yet easy to carry with you. If you're using a fire pan, elevate it slightly on rocks or compacted snow to prevent it from melting into the surface. And when you're done, the ashes are contained within the pan, making it easy to pack them out with you.

A fire blanket is another alternative. It's essentially a heat-resistant cloth that you can lay down on the ground, acting as a buffer between the fire and the earth. Place the blanket on a durable surface, then build a small fire on top. When you're finished, you can shake off the ashes, fold up the blanket, and leave no sign that a fire ever burned there.

For a simpler solution, consider bringing along a Solo Stove. The small Solo Stove Lite model is perfect for cooking, while the larger Solo Stove Titan or Bonfire can create the ambiance of a campfire without the environmental impact. The Solo Stove design is efficient and nearly smokeless, burning fuel more completely than a traditional fire. And when you're finished, there's no fire ring or scorched earth—just a clean space, as if you were never there.

Waste Management in Winter

Whether I'm in a camper or a tent, I'm careful with waste—especially gray water from washing dishes or cleaning gear. In the camper, gray and black water needs to be emptied at designated dump sites. These sites are invaluable, often charging a small fee but worth every penny to keep waste out of the wilderness. For those camping out of a tent, gray water disposal is more about scattering it carefully, far from water sources, to avoid contamination. It's easy to think of winter as a time when "everything's frozen," but when the snow melts, those traces remain. Leaving no trace means thinking ahead and doing everything we can to preserve the landscape in all seasons.

Handling Waste Without a Trace

In winter, waste disposal becomes even more important—and more challenging. Snow and cold temperatures have a way of hiding things, but that doesn't mean they disappear. In fact, organic waste like food scraps or biodegradable items will sit almost unchanged until the thaw. And when spring arrives, they'll reappear as a reminder of every careless drop.

For food waste, pack out everything. Even that handful of crumbs or the peel from your morning orange needs to come back with you. Out there, animals are more likely to be foraging, and human food scraps can disrupt their natural behaviors, making them dependent on or even vulnerable to human food. One spring, I returned to a favorite boondocking spot only to find orange peels, half-buried by melting snow, scattered across the ground. It was a small thing, but seeing those scraps reminded me how even biodegradable waste doesn't disappear in winter—it just waits to reappear in spring. Now, every time I camp in winter, I'm meticulous about packing out every crumb. It's a small effort, but it keeps these places as beautiful as they were when I found them.

For human waste, winter camping requires special considerations. A wag bag—a portable waste bag—is one of the most practical solutions. It's a heavy-duty, sealable bag that contains a powder to neutralize waste and reduce odor. Instead of digging a cathole in frozen ground, you can use a wag bag, seal it up, and pack it out. This way, you're not leaving behind any human waste to thaw and leach into the environment when spring arrives. Wag bags are an easy, responsible solution for preserving the purity of the winter landscape.

If you're in a camper or van and need to dispose of gray water (from washing or cleaning) or black water (from a portable toilet), look for designated dump sites. These sites are designed to handle waste properly, preventing contamination of natural areas. Some charge a small fee, but the convenience and peace of mind are well worth it. By using a proper dump site, you ensure that none of your waste will seep into the ground or harm nearby water sources when the snow melts.

Cooking and Cleaning With Care

Even dishwater can leave a trace in winter. When washing dishes or cookware, strain out any food particles and pack them out. What might seem like a few harmless crumbs can attract wildlife, disrupting their natural diets and routines.

Gray water disposal requires some planning in snowy environments. Avoid pouring gray water in one spot, as it can create a patch of contaminated snow. Instead, disperse it over a wide area, at least 200 feet from any water sources, and ideally on compacted snow or a solid surface to prevent it from pooling. In remote areas, your goal is to minimize any signs of human presence, allowing the landscape to retain its natural state.

Embracing Silence and Solitude

Winter has a quiet that's hard to find any other time of year. Sound carries further in the cold, and the stillness can feel like part of the landscape itself. Out there, loud noises don't just disrupt the peace—they alter the experience of the place. Use headphones if you want to listen to music, or keep your voice low when talking around camp. The solitude of winter is a rare and fragile gift, one that's worth preserving.

One of my favorite memories of winter solitude was standing on the edge of a frozen Bear Lake in Idaho at dusk, with the world wrapped in complete silence. A serene, snow-covered paradise, almost like a scene from a snow globe! The turquoise waters of the lake were partially frozen, creating striking patterns as the ice shifted and captured the light. Snow blanketed the surrounding mountains, adding a soft, sparkling layer over the rolling hills and trees, while the landscape was wonderfully quiet and peaceful. I could hear nothing but my own breathing and the occasional creak of the ice. At that moment, it felt like I was the only person in the world. Moments like that are why I avoid making unnecessary noise in winter—the silence is a gift I don't want to shatter.

If you're lucky enough to encounter wildlife, observe from a distance. Animals are using every bit of energy to survive the winter, and even a slight disturbance can force them to flee, wasting precious calories. Keep your food and scented items secure to avoid drawing them in—bears may be hibernating, but smaller animals like foxes and birds are active and always on the lookout for food.

The Power of Intention

Practicing Leave No Trace in winter isn't about rigid rules—it's about intention. It's about moving through a pristine landscape with respect, knowing that each step leaves an imprint. From where you camp to how you cook, every choice has the power to preserve the quiet beauty around you. By planning ahead, using sustainable tools like wag bags and Solo Stoves, and seeking designated dump sites when needed, you can travel through the winter wilderness without disturbing its delicate balance.

After one particularly cold winter boondocking trip, I remember packing up my camp and looking back at the untouched snow. There were no fire scars, no food scraps, no sign that anyone had been there—except for my footprints and the faint marks from my truck's tires. It felt good to leave the place as pure and quiet as I'd found it, knowing that the next person who stumbled upon it would see only the beauty of winter. Practicing Leave No Trace isn't about following strict rules—it's about honoring the places that give us so much.

Out there, your presence doesn't have to be permanent. Winter's quiet, untouched beauty asks only that you leave it as you found it so that others can experience the same sense of awe and stillness. Leave no trace, and let the land remember you as a respectful guest, one who understood its fragility and chose to tread lightly.

Chapter 9

Creating a Base of Comfort and Security

> *"Comfort in the winter wild is not about luxury—it's about ingenuity, preparation, and knowing how to make the rugged feel like home."*
>
> **—Thom Barrett**

Winter camping is a unique dance with nature—a careful balance of preparation, resilience, and adaptability. For those of us lucky enough to travel with a truck camper, that dance gets a little easier and a bit more comfortable. After years of roughing it in tents, setting up and breaking down camp day after day, I've come to appreciate the value of a camper as a reliable base of operations in the wilderness. I love my setup: a sturdy truck camper as my mobile home, towing my Jeep behind me. The Jeep gives me the freedom to roam and explore while the camper remains my warm, familiar base camp.

The Comforts of a Truck Camper

Waking up to frozen boots and damp sleeping bags during my tent camping days is something I definitely don't miss. In some ways, having a truck camper feels like I'm cheating. I remember one particularly rough night in Montana, where I spent hours battling high winds that seemed determined to tear my tent apart. When I finally upgraded to a truck camper, it felt almost luxurious to have a warm, dry space waiting for me after a long day outdoors. Now, I appreciate those little comforts—a warm bed, dry clothes, and a steady shelter—in a way I never did before. One of the biggest perks? My hiking boots are no longer frozen solid in the mornings; now, they're toasty warm, ready for the day ahead. It's a slight difference, but out there, it feels huge.

Finding the Perfect Campsite

A truck camper changes everything. No more packing up gear in the cold every morning, no more digging around for dry clothes in a damp tent. Instead, everything has its place, ready and waiting for when I return from a long day outdoors. And, unlike a tent that has to be dismantled and moved every time you shift locations, a camper offers a consistent, stable home wherever you choose to park it. For an extended winter trip especially, that consistency makes a tremendous difference.

When I set up camp, I'm deliberate about where I park. In winter, it's worth taking the time to find a sheltered, level spot, ideally with a natural windbreak—a stand of trees or the lee side of a hill. The goal is to be protected from those bitter, relentless winter gusts that can rattle a camper through the night and steal heat faster than you can generate it.

Beyond shelter, I also look for two other critical factors: adequate sunlight for my solar panel and a clear line of sight for my Starlink dish. Solar panels are essential for keeping my batteries charged, powering lights, heating, and electronics. Even in winter, with shorter days, a few hours of good sunlight can make a difference. I try to avoid sites that are completely shaded by trees or rock outcroppings, instead choosing a spot with enough exposure to capture whatever sunlight the day offers.

For those of us relying on Starlink or other satellite internet, a clear view of the sky is equally essential. I check that I have an unobstructed view to the north, where the satellite connection is strongest. If I plan on staying for a few days, this clear line-of-sight means I can stay connected when I need to—whether it's checking the weather forecast, uploading photos, or sending a quick message to family back home.

Once I've found the right place that balances all these factors—shelter from the wind, access to sunlight, and a clear line of sight—I always park with the truck facing out toward the exit route. If there's a heavy snowfall overnight, backing out can be tricky, even with four-wheel drive. Having the truck pointed toward the way out means that if the weather takes a turn, I can simply pull forward and be on my way without maneuvering.

Creating a Drying Area Inside the Camper

Inside the camper, I've created a drying area—a small but crucial feature. There's nothing worse than returning from a day of hiking, snowshoeing, or skiing to find your gear damp and cold with no way to dry it. I set up a drying rack near the heater, a dedicated space for wet clothes, boots, and gear. In a tent, drying anything in winter is nearly impossible, but in the camper, I have the luxury of warmth and space. I can hang up my gloves, socks, and outer layers, and by morning, they're dry and ready to go. It's a minor comfort, but out there, those minor comforts add up to a better night's sleep and a smoother start to the next day.

Cooking Outside to Keep the Camper Fresh

Cooking, too, takes on a different rhythm in a truck camper. In winter, I always prefer to cook outside, even with the camper's built-in kitchen. There's something about the smell of food lingering in a confined space that doesn't sit well with me—especially when I know that food odors can attract wildlife in more remote areas. One evening in Idaho, I made the mistake of cooking inside the camper. I woke up in the middle of the night to scratching sounds outside, and when I peeked out the window, I saw a curious raccoon sniffing around. Since then, I've made it a rule to cook outside, even in the cold—it's a little extra effort, but it keeps the camper smelling neutral and discourages unwanted nighttime visitors.

I set up a small cooking station under a canopy just outside the camper, a spot sheltered enough from the wind to keep the flame steady. If there's snow on the ground, I'll pack it down to make a firm base, sometimes even digging out a small cooking area to protect the stove from gusts. With a Solo Stove for warmth and a small camp stove for cooking, I create a little outdoor kitchen that keeps the camper clean and free of lingering scents. It's practical, but it's also a ritual—a way to enjoy the fresh air and the quiet, even as the sun sets and the cold deepens.

Winter Camping in a Tent: Finding Comfort in the Ruggedness

For those camping in a tent, setting up camp in winter is a more rugged experience, but there's an art to it. Selecting a site becomes as much about survival as comfort. I remember my days of tent camping, searching for that perfect sheltered spot where the wind couldn't whip straight through me in the middle of the night. You learn to look for natural windbreaks—trees, rock outcroppings, or a low dip in the land where you can find some reprieve from the gusts.

Setting Up Your Tent on Snow

If there's deep snow, I'll pack it down or even dig out a small trench to place the tent. This creates a level, insulated surface and a bit of a barrier against the wind. And if it's especially windy, a low snow wall built on the windward side of the tent can make a world of difference. You learn these tricks as you go, small ways to create comfort where none seems to exist.

Layering for Warmth Inside the Tent

Inside the tent, creating warmth is a matter of layering and insulation. Placing an insulated mat under your sleeping bag provides a buffer from the frozen ground, keeping you warmer through the night. And here's a trick for keeping the interior just a bit warmer: dig a small cold sink in the vestibule, a shallow trench where cold air can settle rather than creep into your sleeping space. It's a small touch, but in winter, every degree matters.

Final Thoughts: Respecting the Landscape and Preparing for the Unexpected

The way we set up camp in winter—whether with the relative luxury of a truck camper or the raw simplicity of a tent—reflects our respect for the landscape and our understanding of its challenges. Winter is beautiful, but it's unforgiving. The correct setup means you're prepared for whatever the season brings, whether that's a peaceful evening by a crackling fire or a quick, quiet exit as a snowstorm rolls in. With a bit of planning, a little patience, and the right mindset, you can create a space that's warm, secure, and inviting—a small refuge in the vast, silent beauty of winter.

Chapter 10
The Road Ahead – Embracing Winter's Call

> *"The wilderness doesn't owe you a thing, but if you respect it, it gives you clarity, wonder, and strength no words can capture."*
> —**Thom Barrett**

With my home secured, my vehicle loaded, and my gear packed, I set off into the snow-covered wilderness, ready for whatever the season brings. Every step I've taken in preparation gives me confidence. I know that I'm equipped, self-sufficient, and capable of facing whatever challenges lie ahead. Winter demands respect, but it also offers a thrill that's hard to find elsewhere—a chance to meet nature on its terms and find strength within myself.

Why Winter?

People often ask why I choose to venture out in the winter. My reasons are many, and each one is part of the pull that brings me back to the cold, quiet wild every year. First, I'm an introvert by nature, and I'm happiest when the world around me is calm and still. In summer, trails and campsites can be crowded, full of voices, footsteps, and laughter—all sounds I appreciate but prefer at a distance. Winter camping is an invitation to solitude. Out there in the off-season, I rarely have to worry about parking spots or waiting in line for a view. I can experience the landscape on my own terms, without interruptions, moving through the world at a pace that feels natural to me.

I also love the challenge of winter camping. It's hard, no question about it, and that's part of why it makes me feel so alive. Every trip into the cold demands that I dig deep, rely on my preparation, and stay fully aware of my surroundings. The feeling of satisfaction after a day spent navigating snow-covered trails, setting up camp in freezing temperatures, or melting snow for water is unlike anything else. It's a visceral reminder of what I'm capable of, and even after I return home, I find myself replaying those moments in my mind—the small victories and the obstacles overcome.

And then there's the quiet. In winter, snow blankets the landscape, acting as a natural sound barrier. It absorbs noise, creating a silence that's deeper than any other season can offer. This isn't just quiet—it's absolute, profound stillness, where the loudest sound might be my own breath or the crunch of snow underfoot. In that silence, even the slightest sounds take on meaning. The hoot of an owl in the distance, the howling of coyotes staking their claim, or the soft fall of snow from a branch becomes an entire world of sound. There's a purity to it that's hard to find anywhere else.

And winter brings a certain kind of wildlife encounter that you just don't experience in warmer months. I'll never forget the sight of a bison standing alone in a snowy field, steam rising from its nostrils, icicles clinging to its thick fur, or the quiet struggle of a hare as it bounds across a deep snowdrift. These animals are in their element there, adapted to survive the season's challenges in ways that command respect. Winter reveals a side of the natural world that is raw and unfiltered, where each creature—myself included—exists at the edge of survival and resilience. Watching these animals reminds me of how I, too, am a part of this wilderness, striving to live in harmony with its demands.

Reflecting on the Journey

Preparation is vital to a successful winter trip, but what I do after returning home is just as important. When I come back from the wilderness, I take time to reflect on the journey and capture everything I've learned along the way. I keep a journal specifically for this purpose, noting down the highlights, the problem areas, and any unique challenges I encountered. Each entry is a piece of wisdom that helps me refine my approach, building a personal guidebook of winter's lessons.

This journal isn't just a record of my own experiences. It's also a place to collect insights shared by others—local experts, fellow winter campers, and mentors who've been generous with their advice. Sometimes, the best tips come from those who've walked these trails before me. A suggestion about how to layer more effectively, a warning about a particular trail, or a reminder to always check for avalanche risk—these become part of my developing understanding of winter camping. The knowledge I gather is both individual and communal, woven from my own experiences and those who came before me.

Evaluating and Replenishing Gear

One of the most critical aspects of post-trip preparation is evaluating the gear I used. Winter camping can be harsh on equipment, and some items—like water bottles, batteries, or even food—may freeze or be rendered ineffective by the cold. I check each item carefully to see if anything needs to be cleaned, dried, repaired, or replaced.

If I use emergency supplies or consumables, such as first aid items, snacks, or even duct tape, I make sure to replenish them immediately. Waiting to restock these essentials can be tempting, but neglecting them might mean I forget something vital before my next adventure. By restocking right away, I ensure that my backpack and emergency kit are fully equipped and ready to go.

Certain items, like hand warmers or fire-starting materials, may lose effectiveness over time or after exposure to extreme temperatures. I replace these as needed, ensuring that every piece of gear I might rely on is in top condition. This routine has become second nature, and taking a little time now could prevent a problematic situation down the line.

A Backpack Ready for the Next Trip

Maintaining a ready-to-go backpack is more than a time-saver—it's a safety measure and mental comfort. Each time I head into the wilderness, I'm carrying my lifeline on my back. After every trip, I meticulously organize my pack, refilling used items and ensuring everything's in its place. This habit means that when the next adventure calls, I can grab my backpack with confidence, knowing it's ready for whatever lies ahead.

One outing, however, reminded me how even minor oversights can have significant consequences. I was heading to the Spirit Mountain Cave near Cody, Wyoming—a hidden gem in the Bighorn Basin. After getting the key from the BLM office and notifying them of my plans, I set out with my pack ready and fully stocked with food, clothing, and lighting gear, including a headlamp, a handheld torch, and my phone.

As I entered the cave, the cool air and shadowed walls felt like stepping into another world. The passage descended gradually, with textured limestone walls twisting in ancient patterns. Not far in, the space opened into a vast chamber, where stalactites hung like icy chandeliers, and stalagmites rose in statuesque silence. The quiet was surreal, broken only by the soft drip of water echoing off the walls.

Then, suddenly, my headlamp went out, plunging everything into a pitch-black silence. Startled, I pulled out my handheld torch. The light revealed the path again, but something felt off. Just as I started forward, the torch died, too. No light from the entrance reached me, and with only the sound of dripping water to orient myself, I was alone in an abyss.

I dropped to all fours, using my hands to feel the rocky path. It took a few disorienting minutes before I remembered my phone's flashlight. That light saved me, guiding me safely back out of the cave, but I'd learned my lesson the hard way—always check batteries before a trip.

Now, by organizing my backpack after each outing, I avoid preventable mistakes. My pack has become a trusted companion, equipped and ready, giving me peace of mind and letting me focus on the adventure ahead.

The Cycle of Preparation and Experience

Each winter journey I take is part of a continuous cycle of preparation, experience, reflection, and learning. I know that winter will always have new lessons to teach me, and every trip leaves me a little more in tune with this season's rhythm. Whether it's a better way to set up my shelter, an insight into managing my layers more efficiently, or a reminder to always be vigilant of changing snow conditions, each trip adds to my knowledge.

Winter camping isn't just about braving the cold or surviving the elements—it's about living in harmony with a beautiful and unforgiving landscape. There's a solitude in winter that doesn't exist in any other season. The quiet is deeper, the landscape starker, and the beauty more intense. Every breath of cold air, every step through fresh snow, brings a heightened awareness of being alive. Winter strips things down to their essentials, demanding focus, respect, and a willingness to slow down and listen.

Looking Forward

The wilderness in winter is both a challenge and a gift, offering moments of breathtaking beauty and testing my resilience. Each adventure leaves me with a little more knowledge, a bit more respect for the natural world, and a renewed appreciation for the gear that supports me. With each journey, I come away more equipped—physically, mentally, and emotionally—for the road ahead.

As I put my journal away, replenish my supplies, and store my backpack, I find myself already thinking about the next trip. Winter's call is relentless, and there's always another path to explore, another frozen landscape to discover. I'm ready for whatever lies ahead, knowing that each experience prepares me for the next—not just in the wilderness but in life. Winter camping has taught me patience, resilience, and a deep respect for the world around me, gifts that extend far beyond the trail.

In the end, winter demands respect, preparation, and a willingness to learn. For those who embrace its beauty and challenges, it rewards with an unmatched sense of peace and accomplishment. As I stand on the threshold of each new journey, I feel a little more alive, ready to step once again into the quiet, snow-covered wild. Out there, where nature is both a challenge and a companion, I am reminded of what it truly means to be resilient, to be present, and to live fully in each moment.

Appendices: Various Checklists for Winter Travel

> *"The small things you prepare for are the big things that save your life."*
> **—Thom Barrett**

Appendix A: Home Preparation Checklist for Extended Absence

Appendix B: Must-Have Items Checklist for Boondocking Trips

Appendix C: Detail Checklist for Winter Road Trip

Appendix D: Essential Technologies for Backcountry and Boondocking Adventures

Appendix E: Comprehensive Wilderness First-Aid Kit for Winter Adventures

Appendix F: Apps Used for Planning, Determining Campsites, Navigation, Monitoring Technology, and Ski Mountaineering

Appendix A: Home Preparation Checklist for Extended Absence

1. **Secure the Home**
   o Lock all doors and windows.
   o Ensure the alarm system is activated and functioning, if applicable.
   o Inform a trusted neighbor or friend of your absence and provide emergency contact information.
   o Consider installing motion-detector lights or timed lighting systems to make the home appear occupied.
   o Install security cameras. Consider installing cameras, especially those that allow remote monitoring.
   o Disable garage door opener. Disconnect the garage door opener to prevent unauthorized access.
   o Hide valuables. Move valuable items out of sight from windows or secure them in a safe.

2. **Manage Utilities**
   o Set the thermostat to a temperature that will prevent pipes from freezing (typically no lower than 55°F/13°C).
   o Shut off the main water supply if not needed to prevent flooding and freezing pipes.
   o Unplug all unnecessary appliances to prevent fire hazards and save energy.
   o Stop or forward mail and pause any subscription services.
   o Turn down the water heater. Lower the temperature on your water heater, or turn it off if it's electric, to save energy while you're away.

3. **Prepare for Weather**
   o Clean gutters and downspouts to prevent ice dams or water buildup.
   o Inspect the roof for any damage that could worsen with winter weather.
   o Arrange for snow removal if snowfall is expected during your absence.

- o   Trim trees and branches. Remove any branches that could fall on your home under the weight of snow.

4. **Home Maintenance**
   - o   Dispose of any perishable items in the refrigerator and pantry to prevent odors and pests.
   - o   Remove all trash from the home.
   - o   Check that all smoke and carbon monoxide detectors are functioning, and replace batteries if needed.
   - o   Complete any repairs that could worsen, such as fixing leaks or sealing pest entry points.
   - o   Check for fire hazards. Look for any potential fire hazards (flammable materials, frayed cords) and remove or secure them.
   - o   Test fire extinguishers. Ensure you have accessible, functioning fire extinguishers in the home.

5. **Plumbing & HVAC**
   - o   Add antifreeze to drains and toilets if in a region with freezing temperatures.
   - o   Service your heating system to ensure it runs smoothly during the winter.
   - o   Shut off and drain outdoor faucets to prevent freezing and bursting.
   - o   Open cabinet doors. Leave cabinet doors under sinks open to allow warm air to circulate around pipes, reducing the risk of freezing in colder areas.

6. **Garden and Exterior**
   - o   Store or secure outdoor furniture and loose items that could be moved by storms.
   - o   Cover or store grills and other outdoor cooking appliances.
   - o   Trim trees or branches. Remove any branches that could fall on your home under the weight of snow.

7. **Communication**
   - o   Leave emergency contact information with a neighbor, friend, or family member.
   - o   Ensure someone has a key and knows how to handle potential issues with the home.

- o Provide contact information to the local police department and inform them of your absence (especially in small communities).
- o Schedule regular checks. Ask a neighbor or friend to check the property periodically and pick up any flyers or packages that may get delivered.
- o Provide home instructions. Leave simple instructions for operating essential

8. **Financial and Legal Matters**
   - o Pay any bills due during your absence or set them to be paid automatically.
   - o Notify bank and credit card companies of your travel to prevent fraud alerts.

9. **Insurance**
   - o Confirm your insurance coverage continues uninterrupted while the home is vacant.
   - o Verify any requirements needed to keep your home insured during your absence.

10. **Pest Prevention**
    - o Ensure all food is sealed and stored properly.
    - o Seal cracks or holes on the home exterior to prevent pest entry.
    - o Set up pest traps or schedule a preventative visit from a pest control service.

11. **Electronics and Digital Security**
    - o Secure Wi-Fi network. Ensure your Wi-Fi network is secure (change passwords if needed) to prevent unauthorized access.
    - o Turn off unnecessary devices. In addition to unplugging, make sure all network-connected devices are powered down to prevent unnecessary activity.
    - o Back up important files. If you have critical data at home, back it up to a secure cloud or external storage device in case of power surges or damage.

12. **Vehicle Preparation (if leaving a vehicle behind)**
    o   Store your car in the garage. If possible, park your vehicle in the garage to protect it from the weather and reduce the risk of theft.
    o   Disconnect the battery. If you're leaving for an extended period, disconnect the car battery to prevent it from draining.
    o   Fill the gas tank and check the tires. Fill the gas tank to prevent condensation and check tire pressure, especially in winter.
    o   Arrange for start-up. Ask a neighbor or friend to start the car periodically if it will be idle for a long time to keep the battery charged and prevent engine issues.

13. **Special Considerations for Pets**
    o   Arrange pet care. If you have pets, make arrangements for their care or boarding.
    o   Provide pet-specific instructions. Leave instructions for pet care if a friend or pet sitter is looking after them.

14. **Final Walkthrough**
    o   Do a final walkthrough. Before leaving, walk through each room to make sure everything is unplugged, windows and doors are locked, and all items on your checklist have been completed.
    o   Take photos. Take photos of your home's condition before you leave, including any valuable items. This can be helpful for insurance claims if anything goes wrong while you're away.

By following this checklist, you can have peace of mind knowing that your home is secure, energy-efficient, and well-maintained while you're away for an extended period, especially during the demanding winter months.

Appendix B: Must-Have Items Checklist for Boondocking Trips

Vehicle Equipment
- Reliable Vehicle: Ensure your vehicle is robust and suitable for off-road conditions.
- Spare Tires and Repair Kit: Carry at least one spare tire and tools for basic repairs.
- Recovery Gear: Include a winch, tow straps, and traction mats for getting unstuck.
- Extra Fuel: Bring extra fuel containers for areas with limited fuel stations.

Navigation Tools
- GPS Device and Maps: Have both a GPS device and physical maps as backups.
- Satellite Phone or Communicator: Essential for communication in areas without cell service.

Camping Gear
- Quality Tent and Sleeping Bags: Ensure they are weather-appropriate and durable.
- Portable Stove and Cooking Supplies: Compact and easy to use for cooking meals.
- Water Purification System: To provide safe drinking water if supplies run low.
- Solar Charger or Portable Generator: For powering electronic devices off-grid.

Food and Water Supplies
- Non-Perishable Food: Enough to last until the next resupply point.
- Adequate Water Storage: Large, durable containers to store sufficient drinking water.
- Cooler or Portable Fridge: To keep perishables fresh for longer.

Clothing and Personal Items
- o Layered Clothing: Adaptable to changing weather conditions.
- o First Aid Kit: Comprehensive and tailored to the group's needs.
- o Personal Hygiene Products: Biodegradable soap, toothpaste, and other essentials.

Emergency and Safety Gear
- o Fire Extinguisher: Ensure it's suitable for vehicle and campsite fires.
- o Emergency Beacon or Locator: Critical for alerting rescue services in emergencies.
- o Comprehensive Tool Kit: Contains tools for any necessary repairs or adjustments.

Entertainment and Leisure
- o Books, Games, and Downloaded Entertainment: For downtime and relaxation.
- o Camera or GoPro: To document your adventures and capture memories.

Appendix C: Detail Checklist for Winter Road Trip

1. **Winter-Ready Vehicle**
    - **Dual Batteries with Isolator**: Ensure dual battery setup with a battery isolator to prevent one battery from draining the other.
    - **Vehicle Service**: Verify the vehicle is fully serviced and winter-ready.
    - **Antifreeze Check**: Check and refill antifreeze to prevent freezing.
    - **Well-Charged Batteries**: Ensure both batteries are charged and in good condition for cold starts.
    - **Winter Tires and Chains**: Equip vehicles with winter tires and carry chains for better traction.
    - **Half-Full Gas Tank**: Keep the gas tank at least half-full to avoid gas line freeze-up; use gas line antifreeze as needed.
    - **Spare Tire and Tire Repair Kit**: Confirm a usable spare tire and carry a tire repair kit and portable air compressor.
    - **Windshield Washer Fluid**: Use winter-grade washer fluid and carry an extra bottle.
    - **Spare Fuses**: Pack spare fuses for essential systems (lights, heater, etc.).
    - **Engine Block Heater**: If available, ensure it's functional for easier starts in extreme cold.

2. **Emergency Roadside Kit**
    - Jumper cables or portable jump starter.
    - Flares or reflective triangles.
    - Ice scraper and brush.
    - Shovel and ax for clearing snow or debris on remote roads.
    - Tow rope or chain.
    - Winch (if installed, check it's operational).
    - Fuel additives (to prevent fuel from gelling in extreme cold).

3. **Basic Tools**
    - **Multi-Tool or Knife**: For various roadside needs.
    - **Screwdrivers**:
      Flathead (slotted).

Phillips.
Posidrive.
Torx (star).
Hex (Allen).
Square (Robertson).
Tri-Wing.
Torq-set.
- **Torque Wrench**: Essential for checking lug nuts on tires.
- **Pliers**: Standard, needle-nose, and vice grips.
- **Adjustable Wrench**: For various nuts and bolts.
- **Socket Set**: Includes both metric and imperial sizes.
- **Hammer**: For minor repairs or breaking ice.
- **Tire Pressure Gauge**: To maintain correct tire pressure in fluctuating winter temperatures.
- **Tow Strap or Rope**: For pulling vehicles out of snow.
- **Duct Tape and Cable Ties**: For temporary repairs.
- **Flashlight and Extra Batteries**: For low-light situations.
- **Shovel**: Compact, foldable shovel for digging out of snow.
- **Gloves and Hand Cleaner**: Protect hands and clean up after repairs.

4. **Winter Survival Kit**
   - Extra winter clothing and blankets.
   - Thermal emergency blanket or space blanket.
   - Hand and foot warmers.
   - Waterproof matches and whistle.
   - High-energy food supply (like energy bars).
   - Extra water (insulated to avoid freezing).

5. **Snow Removal Tools**
   - High-quality ice scraper.
   - Snowbrush.
   - Small, collapsible shovel.

6. **Traction Aids**
   - **Traction Pads**: For placing under wheels to gain traction in snow, ice, sand, or mud.
     - Easy to use and safe.

- Lightweight and portable.
- Durable and cost-effective.
o Multipurpose use (can also serve as a shovel or jack base).

7. **Communication and Navigation Tools**
   o **Charged Cell Phone and Charger**: Keep phone charged; bring a car charger or portable power bank.
   o **Emergency Radio**: Battery-powered or hand-crank radio to stay updated on weather.
   o **Satellite Communicator**: For remote areas with no cell service (e.g., Garmin inReach).
   o **CB Radio**: For communicating in remote areas with no cell signal.
   o **Physical Maps**: Bring printed maps as backup in case GPS is unavailable.
   o **Compass**: Analog compass for basic navigation backup.

8. **First-Aid Kit**
   o Stocked with essentials for minor injuries, including any necessary medications. (See Appendix E for a detailed wilderness first-aid kit.)

9. **Personal Safety and Comfort**
   o **Personal Locator Beacon (PLB)**: For remote wilderness areas to alert rescue services if needed.
   o **Fire Extinguisher**: Small, vehicle-rated extinguisher for engine or electrical fires.
   o **Portable Camping Stove**: Compact stove with fuel canister for emergency heating or melting snow.
   o **Emergency Shelter**: Portable shelter (e.g., tent or bivy sack) in case of leaving vehicle.
   o **Waterproof Storage Bags**: Organize and protect important items, especially electronics and first-aid supplies.

10. **Vehicle Condition Checks Before Departure**
    o **Battery Condition**: Confirm full charge and inspect terminals for corrosion.
    o **Brake Fluid and Power Steering Fluid**: Ensure both are topped up and winter-ready.

- o **Inspect Wiper Blades**: Use winter-grade blades for snowy or icy conditions.
- o **Lubricate Door Locks and Hinges**: Apply silicone-based lubricant to prevent freezing.
- o **Inspect Belts and Hoses**: Check for wear or cracks, as cold can damage rubber components.

11. **Extra Health and Safety Supplies**
    - o Extra medications.
    - o Sunscreen and lip balm to protect from snow glare.
    - o Trash bags for waste, waterproofing items, or emergency insulation.

12. **Warm Clothing and Blankets**
    - o Extra gloves, hats, scarves, thermal socks, and enough blankets or sleeping bags for all passengers.

13. **Sunglasses**
    - o Protect against snow glare with polarized sunglasses.

14. **Water and Snacks**
    - o Bring water and non-perishable snacks that don't need heating in case of delays or being stranded.

15. **Final Preparation Before Heading Out**
    - o **Check the Weather and Road Conditions**: Confirm expected conditions and adjust plans as needed.
    - o **Inform Someone of Your Plans**: Share your route and estimated arrival time with a friend or family member.
    - o **Test All Electronics**: Verify flashlights, GPS, phone chargers, and other electronics are in working order.
    - o **Run the Vehicle for a Short Trip**: Take a quick drive to test winter readiness.
    - o **Plan for Extra Time**: Allow for slower travel and frequent breaks; don't rush.
    - o **Mental Preparedness**: Review safety protocols and mentally prepare for possible isolation or delays.

Appendix D: Essential Technologies for Backcountry and Boondocking Adventures

Below is a curated list of gadgets and technologies I have found invaluable during my travels in remote and backcountry areas. These items enhance safety, connectivity, and comfort, ensuring a reliable and enjoyable experience.

1. **Cell Boosters**
   weBoost Drive X
   - **Purpose:** To enhance cell signals in vehicles.
   - **Key Features:**
     - Compatible with all U.S. carriers; supports 4G LTE and 5G.
     - Magnetic roof antenna for easy setup.
     - Designed for reliable signal boosting while driving through remote areas.
   - **Why It's Useful:** It ensures reliable communication off-grid.
   - **Pro Tip:** Use it with a GPS device for seamless navigation and communication.

2. **Satellite Communication**
   Garmin inReach Mini
   - **Purpose:** A compact satellite communicator for remote communication and navigation.
   - **Key Features:**
     - Two-way messaging via the Iridium satellite network.
     - SOS button for emergencies, connecting to a 24/7 monitoring center.
     - GPS navigation with tracking and route planning.
   - **Why It's Useful:** It's essential for solo travelers in areas without cell service.
   - **Pro Tip:** Pair it with the Garmin Explore app for enhanced map functionality.

   Starlink
   - **Purpose:** A satellite internet provider for remote areas.
   - **Key Features:**

- o High-speed internet access even in isolated locations.
- o Portable and easy setup with a compact dish and router.
- o Supports video calls, streaming, and other internet-dependent activities.
- **Why It's Useful:** It enables connectivity where traditional internet options are unavailable.
- **Pro Tip:** Set up your Starlink dish in a clear, open area for optimal signal.

3. **Handheld GPS Devices**
   Garmin eTrex 22x and 32x
   - **Purpose:** A rugged, waterproof handheld GPS device for outdoor adventures.
   - **Key Features:**
     - o Preloaded TopoActive maps for navigation.
     - o GPS and GLONASS satellite support for accuracy.
     - o Compact, lightweight design for portability.
   - **Why It's Useful:** It's a reliable navigation in harsh winter conditions.
   - **Pro Tip:** Download maps of your travel area beforehand to avoid connectivity issues.

   Garmin GPSMAP 67i
   I have not used this product; however, it does combine the inReach and GPS together.
   - **Purpose:** High-performance GPS with integrated satellite communication.
   - **Key Features:**
     - o Large, bright display for all lighting conditions.
     - o Multiband technology for enhanced accuracy in dense forests or canyons.
     - o Offers inReach capabilities for communication and SOS features.
   - **Why It's Useful:** It combines GPS navigation with satellite communication for versatile use.
   - **Pro Tip:** Use lithium batteries for cold-weather performance.

4. **Portable Heaters**
   Mr. Heater Portable Buddy
   - **Purpose:** A portable propane heater for outdoor warmth.
   - **Key Features:**
     - Adjustable heat output (4,000 to 9,000 BTU).
     - Heats spaces up to 225 sq ft.
     - Safety shut-off features for tip-over or low oxygen levels.
   - **Why It's Useful:** Reliable heat during cold-weather camping.
   - **Pro Tip:** Ensure proper ventilation to prevent carbon monoxide buildup.

   Mr. Heater Little Buddy
   - **Purpose:** A compact propane heater for smaller spaces.
   - **Key Features:**
     - Outputs 3,800 BTU.
     - Simple on/off button.
     - Lightweight and portable design.
   - **Why It's Useful:** It's ideal for minimalist trips.
   - **Pro Tip:** Combine it with a reflective blanket to maximize heat retention.

5. **Camp Stoves**
   Coleman Classic Propane Stove
   - **Purpose:** Reliable dual-burner stove for camping.
   - **Key Features:**
     - Two adjustable burners.
     - Wind-blocking panels for efficient cooking in breezy conditions.
     - Durable design for long-term use.
   - **Why It's Useful:** It's perfect for group camping.
   - **Pro Tip:** Use propane cylinders with built-in regulators for consistent cold-weather performance.

   MSR WindBurner Stove System
   - **Purpose:** A compact, windproof stove for solo or group backpacking.
   - **Key Features:**
     - Radiant burner technology for fast boil times.

- o Integrated cooking pot with heat exchanger.
- o Compact nesting design for easy packing.
- **Why It's Useful:** Provides efficient cooking in windy environments.
- **Pro Tip:** Pair it with MSR low-temperature fuel canisters for optimal performance.

6. **Fire Pits**
   Solo Stove Bonfire
   - **Purpose:** A mid-sized smokeless fire pit for backyard or car camping.
   - **Key Features:**
     - o Double-wall design for smokeless combustion.
     - o Durable stainless steel construction.
     - o Portable design (weighs 20 lbs).
     - o Efficient wood burning with minimal ash production.
   - **Why It's Useful:** It offers warmth and ambiance without smoke.
   - **Pro Tip:** Use dry, seasoned hardwood for the best performance.

   Solo Stove Lite
   - **Purpose:** Ultra-lightweight stove for hikers and backpackers.
   - **Key Features:**
     - o Compact and lightweight (9 oz).
     - o Burns twigs, leaves, and pinecones; compatible with the Solo Stove Alcohol Burner.
     - o Double-wall construction for efficient, smokeless combustion.
   - **Why It's Useful:** It's a reliable cooking solution without heavy fuel.
   - **Pro Tip:** Collect dry fuel in advance to ensure a quick, efficient burn.

Appendix E: Comprehensive Wilderness First-Aid Kit for Winter Adventures

In winter, the stakes are higher. Cold conditions, delayed medical response times, and the unique challenges of maintaining warmth and mobility mean that every item in your wilderness first-aid kit must pull double duty. This guide integrates essential supplies and explains why each is particularly critical for winter adventures.

1. **Basic First-Aid Supplies**
   Adhesive Bandages (Assorted Sizes)
   - **Purpose**: Protects minor cuts and abrasions from dirt and infection.
   - **Why It's Important in Winter**:
     o Cold air and dry conditions can cause your skin to crack, increasing vulnerability to infection.
     o Snow, ice, and debris can contaminate wounds more easily.
   - **Pro Tip**: Use waterproof bandages to ensure adhesion in wet or snowy environments.

   Sterile Gauze Pads (Various Sizes)
   - **Purpose**: Covers larger wounds, absorbs blood, and prevents infection.
   - **Why It's Important in Winter**:
     o Essential for creating layers of protection in freezing conditions, where blood flow may slow, and wounds take longer to heal.
   - **Pro Tip**: Store gauze in a sealed, waterproof bag to keep it sterile.

   Adhesive Medical Tape
   - **Purpose**: Secures gauze or splints and provides temporary repairs.
   - **Why It's Important in Winter**:
     o It can hold together makeshift insulation for wounds exposed to the cold.

    o   Adhesion may weaken in freezing temperatures, so warming the tape before use is critical.
- **Pro Tip**: Pre-cut strips and store them in an easily accessible container.

Elastic Bandage (ACE)
- **Purpose**: Provides support for sprains and reduces swelling.
- **Why It's Important in Winter**:
    o   Cold temperatures can exacerbate stiffness in sprains, making immediate immobilization even more necessary.
- **Pro Tip**: Wrap lightly to allow circulation, especially in extremities prone to frostbite.

Antiseptic Wipes
- **Purpose**: Cleans wounds and prevents infection.
- **Why It's Important in Winter**:
    o   Snow and ice introduce bacteria to wounds, even when they appear clean.
    o   Freezing temperatures can make water inaccessible for washing wounds.
- **Pro Tip**: Keep wipes close to your body to prevent freezing.

2. **Wound Care**
Wound Irrigation Syringe
- **Purpose**: Flushes dirt and debris from deeper wounds.
- **Why It's Important in Winter**:
    o   Icy conditions often lead to falls that can cause abrasions contaminated with snow and dirt.
- **Pro Tip**: Use warm water for irrigation to avoid additional cooling of the injured area.

Hemostatic Agent (Powder or Gauze)
- **Purpose**: Quickly stops heavy bleeding.
- **Why It's Important in Winter**:
    o   Prevents rapid heat loss from blood loss, which can worsen hypothermia.
- **Pro Tip**: Familiarize yourself with the application process beforehand.

Hydrogel Dressing
- **Purpose**: Treats burns, abrasions, or blisters.
- **Why It's Important in Winter**:
  o Cold and friction from winter boots often cause skin damage that needs moisture to heal.
- **Pro Tip**: Keep dressings in a waterproof container to prevent freezing.

Butterfly Closures
- **Purpose**: Holds small, clean wounds together.
- **Why It's Important in Winter**:
  o Essential for the quick closure of wounds to minimize exposure to the elements.
- **Pro Tip**: Practice applying closures with gloves to simulate real conditions.

3. **Tools and Instruments**

Tweezers
- **Purpose**: Removes splinters, debris, or ticks.
- **Why It's Important in Winter**:
  o Frozen debris or wood shards from collecting firewood are common hazards.
- **Pro Tip**: Choose fine-point tweezers for precision.

Scissors
- **Purpose**: Cuts gauze, tape, or clothing to access wounds.
- **Why It's Important in Winter**:
  o Necessary for cutting through thick winter clothing to reach injuries.
- **Pro Tip**: Blunt-tip scissors are safer for chaotic situations.

Thermometer
- **Purpose**: Monitors body temperature for hypothermia or fever.
- **Why It's Important in Winter**:
  o Critical for detecting early-stage hypothermia, which may present subtly.
- **Pro Tip**: Opt for a digital thermometer designed for extreme temperatures.

Multitool
- **Purpose**: Versatile tool for cutting, gripping, and repairs.
- **Why It's Important in Winter**:
  o   Useful for creating splints, repairing gear, and handling frozen zippers or buckles.
- **Pro Tip**: Ensure it has locking blades for safety during use.

4. **Cold-Weather Specific Supplies**
   Chemical Hand and Toe Warmers
   - **Purpose**: Provides immediate warmth to extremities.
   - **Why It's Important in Winter**:
     o   Prevents frostbite and helps maintain dexterity in freezing conditions.
   - **Pro Tip**: Activate warmers before your extremities feel numb.

   Space Blanket or Emergency Bivvy
   - **Purpose**: Retains body heat to prevent hypothermia.
   - **Why It's Important in Winter**:
     o   Compact and lightweight, these are lifesaving in sudden weather changes or emergencies.
   - **Pro Tip**: Wrap tightly around the core for maximum heat retention.

   Frostbite Cream or Gel
   - **Purpose**: Treat early frostbite symptoms by soothing damaged skin.
   - **Why It's Important in Winter**:
     o   Cold exposure can damage skin layers, and immediate care prevents worsening.
   - **Pro Tip**: Warm the cream before application for better absorption.

5. **Specialized Winter Care**
   Sling
   - **Purpose**: Supports and immobilizes arm or shoulder injuries.
   - **Why It's Important in Winter**:
     o   Reduces strain on injuries during treks, especially when carrying gear.

- o Prevents cold exposure to the injured limb by stabilizing it close to the body.
- **Pro Tip**: Practice creating a sling with a triangular bandage or improvised materials.

Tourniquet
- **Purpose**: Controls severe bleeding.
- **Why It's Important in Winter**:
  - o Prevents life-threatening blood loss, which exacerbates hypothermia in cold conditions.
- **Pro Tip**: Learn to apply a tourniquet while wearing gloves for real-life conditions.

6. **Emergency Items**
Whistle
- **Purpose**: Attracts attention in emergencies.
- **Why It's Important in Winter**:
  - o Audible signals travel further in snow-covered terrain, where visibility is often reduced.
- **Pro Tip**: Use three blasts as a universal distress signal.

Notepad and Waterproof Pen
- **Purpose**: Records injury details or creates notes for rescuers.
- **Why It's Important in Winter**:
  - o Essential when electronics fail due to cold or moisture.
- **Pro Tip**: Write notes about symptoms and time of injury for medical professionals.

Emergency Items
- **Whistle**: To signal for help in an emergency.
- **Notepad and Waterproof Pen**: This is used to record injury details and vital signs.
- **First-Aid Manual**: A small, lightweight guide for reference.
- **Duct Tape**: Multipurpose for temporary repairs or splinting.
- **Matches or Lighter** (stored in a waterproof case): For warmth or signaling.

Personal Items
- **Medical Information Card**: Includes personal medical conditions, allergies, and emergency contact information.
- **Personal Medications**: In labeled, waterproof containers.
- **Extra Pair of Gloves**: Insulated and sterile for cold protection during treatment.

Packing and Organization Tips
- **Waterproof, Durable First-Aid Kit Bag**: Use a durable, sealed container to keep all items dry and accessible with compartments for organization.
- **Organization**: Group items by category for easy access in emergencies.
- **Cold Preparation**: Test handling items with gloves to simulate real conditions.
- **Ziploc Bags**: These are used to store smaller items and keep them dry.
- **Labels**: Clearly mark sections for quick access (e.g., medications, wound care).

Tips for Winter First-Aid Preparedness
1. **Know How to Use the Supplies**: Take a wilderness first-aid course to familiarize yourself with items and their uses.
2. **Repack Before Each Trip**: Ensure nothing has expired or been used.
3. **Adapt for the Group Size and Trip Length**: Scale the kit based on the number of people and the duration of your trip.
4. **Consider Hypothermia Risks**: Be prepared for prolonged cold exposure with additional warming supplies.
5. **Practice Emergency Scenarios**: Simulate using the kit in cold, gloved conditions to ensure efficiency in real situations.

This fully detailed list ensures that your wilderness first-aid kit is comprehensive, with each item tailored to address the challenges of winter travel. Proper preparation is essential to ensure safety, comfort, and effective response in cold-weather emergencies.

Appendix F: Apps Used for Planning, Determining Campsites, Navigation, Monitoring Technology, and Ski Mountaineering

1. **Boondocking and Campsite Finder Apps**
   - **iOverlander**
     - **Purpose:** Locate free and paid camping spots, including boondocking sites.
     - **Summary:** A community-driven app for finding camping locations worldwide.
     - **Platforms:** iOS, Android, Web.
     - **Where to Obtain:** iOS App Store | Google Play Store | Official Website.
     - **Winter Usefulness:** Identifies year-round campsites, ideal for boondocking in remote areas.

   - **Campendium**
     - **Purpose:** Discover RV parks, campgrounds, and boondocking spots.
     - **Summary:** A comprehensive tool to locate campsites with user reviews and filters.
     - **Platforms:** iOS, Web.
     - **Where to Obtain:** iOS App Store | Official Website.
     - **Winter Usefulness:** Provides detailed insights on campsite accessibility during harsh weather.

   - **The Dyrt**
     - **Purpose:** Find and review campgrounds.
     - **Summary:** A directory of campgrounds with user reviews, photos, and offline capabilities.
     - **Platforms:** iOS, Android, Web.
     - **Where to Obtain:** iOS App Store | Google Play Store | Official Website.
     - **Winter Usefulness:** Offline maps help locate campgrounds in areas with poor connectivity.

- **Boondocking**
  - **Purpose:** Find free camping locations on public lands.
  - **Summary:** A simple app focused on free dispersed camping spots.
  - **Platforms:** iOS, Android.
  - **Where to Obtain:** iOS App Store | Google Play Store.
  - **Winter Usefulness:** Highlights dispersed camping options in areas less affected by winter closures.

- **AllStays**
  - **Purpose:** Provide information on campgrounds, RV parks, and services.
  - **Summary:** An all-in-one camping directory with extensive filters and offline access.
  - **Platforms:** iOS, Web.
  - **Where to Obtain:** iOS App Store | Official Website.
  - **Winter Usefulness:** Filters help find open locations, even in winter.

2. **Navigation and Topographical Map Apps**
   - **Avenza Maps**
     - **Purpose:** Access detailed offline topographical maps.
     - **Summary:** A map app with GPS tracking and annotation capabilities.
     - **Platforms:** iOS, Android.
     - **Where to Obtain:** iOS App Store | Google Play Store | Official Website.
     - **Winter Usefulness:** Essential for navigating remote trails where snow may obscure paths.

   - **onX Offroad**
     - **Purpose:** Navigate off-road trails and public lands.
     - **Summary:** A trail guide app for off-road adventures with terrain insights.
     - **Platforms:** iOS, Android.
     - **Where to Obtain:** iOS App Store | Google Play Store | Official Website.
     - **Winter Usefulness:** Helps identify safe and accessible winter off-road trails.

- **AllTrails**
    - **Purpose:** Discover and navigate hiking, biking, and outdoor trails.
    - **Summary:** A trail database with user reviews, photos, and offline maps.
    - **Platforms:** iOS, Android, Web.
    - **Where to Obtain:** iOS App Store | Google Play Store | Official Website.
    - **Winter Usefulness:** Offers updates on trail conditions during snow-covered months.

- **Trails Offroad**
    - **Purpose:** Provide off-road trail guides.
    - **Summary:** Offers detailed descriptions, GPS tracks, and ratings for off-road trails.
    - **Platforms:** iOS, Android, Web.
    - **Where to Obtain:** iOS App Store | Google Play Store | Official Website.
    - **Winter Usefulness:** Helps find winter-accessible trails for 4x4 or AWD vehicles.

- **Hiking Project**
    - **Purpose:** Provide a comprehensive guide for hiking trails.
    - **Summary:** Features elevation profiles, offline maps, and detailed trail information.
    - **Platforms:** iOS, Android, Web.
    - **Where to Obtain:** iOS App Store | Google Play Store | Official Website.
    - **Winter Usefulness:** Ideal for planning snowshoeing or winter hiking routes.

- **Earthmate**
    - **Purpose:** Pair with Garmin devices for navigation.
    - **Summary:** Provides GPS navigation and topographical maps for remote areas.
    - **Platforms:** iOS, Android.
    - **Where to Obtain:** iOS App Store | Google Play Store | Official Website.

- o **Winter Usefulness:** Ensures reliable navigation in areas with limited connectivity.

- **Gaia GPS**
  - o **Purpose:** Provide topographical maps and route planning tools.
  - o **Summary:** Offers offline maps and multiple data sources for detailed navigation.
  - o **Platforms:** iOS, Android, Web.
  - o **Where to Obtain:** iOS App Store | Google Play Store | Official Website.
  - o **Winter Usefulness:** Essential for navigating areas with heavy snow or challenging terrain.

- **onX Backcountry**
  - o **Purpose:** Provide GPS navigation for hiking, backpacking, and backcountry skiing.
  - o **Summary:** Includes avalanche forecasts, snow depth, and slope angle tools.
  - o **Platforms:** iOS, Android.
  - o **Where to Obtain:** iOS App Store | Google Play Store | Official Website.
  - o **Winter Usefulness:** Specialized for winter safety in backcountry skiing.

3. **Trip Planning and Organization Tools**
   - **Roadtrippers**
     - o **Purpose:** Plan and map road trips with points of interest.
     - o **Summary:** A road trip planner with routes, attractions, and fuel cost estimations.
     - o **Platforms:** iOS, Android, Web.
     - o **Where to Obtain:** iOS App Store | Google Play Store | Official Website.
     - o **Winter Usefulness:** Assists with route adjustments based on winter weather closures.

   - **TripIt**
     - o **Purpose:** Organize travel itineraries.

- o **Summary:** Consolidates all travel details into a single accessible app.
- o **Platforms:** iOS, Android, Web.
- o **Where to Obtain:** iOS App Store | Google Play Store | Official Website.
- o **Winter Usefulness:** Helps accommodate sudden changes due to winter weather.

- **RV LIFE Trip Wizard**
  - o **Purpose:** Plan RV-friendly routes and locate campgrounds.
  - o **Summary:** Customizable route planner with campground reviews and RV-safe navigation.
  - o **Platforms:** iOS, Android, Web.
  - o **Where to Obtain:** iOS App Store | Google Play Store | Official Website.
  - o **Winter Usefulness:** Ensures safe routes and available camping spots during colder months.

4. **Monitoring and Camper System Apps**

- **RV Whisper**
  - o **Purpose:** Monitor RV systems remotely.
  - o **Summary:** Tracks battery, propane, and temperature levels in your RV.
  - o **Platforms:** iOS, Android, Web.
  - o **Where to Obtain:** Official Website.
  - o **Winter Usefulness:** Prevents system failures like frozen pipes by offering real-time alerts.

- **VictronConnect**
  - o **Purpose:** Monitor and configure Victron Energy products.
  - o **Summary:** Real-time monitoring of battery status, solar input, and inverters.
  - o **Platforms:** iOS, Android.
  - o **Where to Obtain:** iOS App Store | Google Play Store.
  - o **Winter Usefulness:** Helps manage power needs, which is crucial in cold weather.

- **SensorPush**
  - **Purpose:** Monitor temperature and humidity levels.
  - **Summary:** Wireless sensors with alerts for critical temperature thresholds.
  - **Platforms:** iOS, Android.
  - **Where to Obtain:** iOS App Store | Google Play Store.
  - **Winter Usefulness:** Maintains safe interior conditions during freezing temperatures.

5. **Ski Mountaineering and Backcountry Skiing Apps**
   - **FATMAP**
     - **Purpose:** Deliver detailed 3D maps for outdoor activities like ski mountaineering.
     - **Summary:** High-resolution maps, terrain analysis, route planning, and offline access.
     - **Platforms:** iOS, Android, Web.
     - **Where to Obtain:** Official Website.
     - **Winter Usefulness:** Helps analyze slopes and routes for safety in winter conditions.

   - **Powder Project**
     - **Purpose:** A community-driven platform to discover ski lines and backcountry routes.
     - **Summary:** User-submitted trail maps, difficulty ratings, and offline access.
     - **Platforms:** iOS, Android, Web.
     - **Where to Obtain:** Official Website.
     - **Winter Usefulness:** Offers detailed ski routes updated by users with local knowledge.

6. **Portable Solar Panels**
   Renogy E.FLEX 10W Solar Panel
   - **Purpose:** Portable solar panel for charging USB devices during outdoor activities.
   - **Key Features:**
     - High-efficiency monocrystalline cells.
     - Lightweight and compact design (13 oz).

- o   Durable, water-resistant construction.
- o   Flexible mounting options (carabiners, suction cups).
- o   Auto-optimization for interrupted charging due to shade or clouds.
- **Why It's Useful:** Reliable power source for gadgets in remote areas.
- **Pro Tip:** Pair it with a portable power bank for energy storage during nighttime or cloudy weather.

About the Author

For over 30 years, I've been tested by Mother Nature, facing her extremes as I ventured deep into the rugged backcountry, boondocking and ski-mountaineering through some of the most remote and challenging landscapes in North America and Europe. Some of these trips veered into complete chaos, moments when weather or terrain threw everything into disarray. My ability to share these stories today is a testament to learning how to slow down, stay calm, and lean into unexpected challenges—skills that only years in the wilderness can truly teach.

My journeys have taken me as far north as Deadhorse, Alaska, into the heart of the Yukon's wilderness, through the towering peaks of British Columbia's Rogers Pass, across the vast, untamed stretches of Idaho, Washington, Oregon, Utah, Montana, Wyoming, and Colorado. From high alpine ridges to dense forests and sweeping valleys, I've made it a mission to venture beyond the well-trodden paths and explore the wild places that others mostly only dream of.

Over the years, I've become proficient in skills essential for survival and navigation in harsh, unpredictable environments, including avalanche safety, ice river crossings, and advanced wilderness first aid. My skills have been tested in everything from unexpected blizzards in Wyoming's Medicine Bow Mountains, where swirling snow and misty peaks transform familiar trails into a winter labyrinth, to whiteouts on the slopes of Alaska's Chugach Mountains. Each of these experiences has reinforced the importance of preparation, adaptability, and respect for the wilderness.

I've built my overlanding rig to be my home on wheels, a reliable companion that has carried me through snow-packed trails, across icy rivers, and over rugged mountain passes. Over the years, I've customized every inch of my rig to handle the extremes of winter overlanding—from the frigid nights in the Yukon to the steep ascents of Montana's snowy passes. One of my most memorable journeys was a seven-month overlanding expedition I called *Chasing My Northern Lights,* where I traveled deep into the Canadian and Alaskan wilderness. Those nights spent under a vast sky, with shooting stars and full moons, were moments of pure wonder and solitude that reminded me why I seek these wild places—to reconnect with something larger than myself.

Throughout my years of exploration, I've developed a deep respect for the skills and knowledge needed to travel safely in these environments. I hold certifications from respected wilderness and survival organizations, including the National Outdoor Leadership School (NOLS) and Wilderness Medicine Institute (WMI), where I completed training as a Wilderness First Responder. These are not just academic credentials; they're the hands-on skills needed to treat injuries, assess avalanche risks, and make sound decisions in some of the harshest conditions imaginable. I consider it my duty to practice and promote Leave No Trace principles, ensuring that these wild places remain pristine for future generations.

My experiences—combined with my formal training—make me an authority on overlanding and backcountry travel. I've learned, often through trial and error, what it takes to thrive in remote settings, where self-sufficiency is essential, and each decision can have serious consequences, like the time I underestimated the cold on a trip through the Yukon and had to adapt quickly to stay warm and safe. Each misstep has taught me something invaluable about preparation and adaptability. One lesson that stands out came during a sudden snowstorm in Rogers Pass, where I had to rely on my wits and my gear to make it through the night. That experience taught me that resilience is as much about mental preparedness as it is about physical strength.

Now, as I share my insights, I hope to inspire others to venture beyond the familiar, to experience the power of the wild firsthand, and to do so with respect, preparation, and a healthy respect for the risks involved. This book is my way of passing on the lessons I've gathered from years of exploration—lessons that are as much about inner strength as they are about physical endurance. Whether you're a seasoned adventurer or someone setting foot into the wild for the first time, I hope these stories and insights encourage you to step outside with confidence, curiosity, and respect for the land.

www.ingramcontent.com/pod-product-compliance
Lightning Source LLC
Chambersburg PA
CBHW060513030426
42337CB00015B/1879